The

Pamphleteers

The Birth of Journalism
Emergence of the Press,
& the Fourth Estate

James A. Oliver

IÅ

2010 & 2017

First Published in the United Kingdom 2010
INFORMATION ARCHITECTS
"IA"
www.IAimprint.com

Worldwide distribution by Ingram Book Group, LLC, USA
www.IngramBook.com

Paperback Edition
ISBN: 978-0-9551834-4-7
Hardback Edition
ISBN: 978-0-9551834-5-4
Illustrated Edition with Archive:
ISBN: 978-0-9556638-7-1

British Library Cataloguing in Publication Data.
A catalogue record for this book is available from the
British Library.

Classification
Non-Fiction:
Early Journalism/Pamphlets & Pamphleteers
Literary Biography/Revolutionary History

BIC Codes:
DSK, BGL, HBTV, KNTJ

1 2 1 1 2 0 1 7 - 0 5
Typeset in Century

Bibliographic Data
www.thepamphleteers.com

The Pamphleteers
James A. Oliver

The Pamphleteers is an investigation of the early journalism and the emergence of the periodical press as the 'fourth estate'.

In an era long before the advent of the 'News Paper', the pamphleteers were the world's proto-journalists. As a paper platform for a spectrum of religious fanatics, eccentrics, social reporters and satirists, the pamphlet also evolved as a weapon of propaganda (forged between the fledgling press and Star Chamber censorship) for powerful vested interests, political elites, governments - and revolutionists.

The Gutenberg revolution-in-print of the Renaissance provided the spark, and the Reformation of the sixteenth century the fuel, for the explosion of the pamphleteering phenomenon. As the pamphlet form took root, then so English prose emerged from its antique form with an extraordinary rash of stylistic innovations to embrace such unlikely postures as subversive fulmination, cod polemic, ferocious satire, and even manifesto.

In times of religious ferment, civil war, colonial unrest and revolution, such texts - risky or even dangerous to publish - were often the product of secret presses and anonymous authors.

At the other exposure, there were those who encountered that risk - and found notoriety or lasting fame along the way. In the hands of a select few, the pamphlet reached a level of high achievement beyond any ordinary Grub Street reckoning.

In this brief survey, the author provides an overview of the timeline from Gutenberg to the French Revolution, with vignettes on: Robert Greene, Thomas Nashe, Thomas Dekker, John Milton, Daniel Defoe, Jonathan Swift, and culminating with the high achievement of Tom Paine.

As a special focus, the narrative reveals how the early journalists were driven, not merely by scandal and sensationalism, but by major historical events on the world stage.

The Pamphleteers is itself a pamphlet for the digital age.

James A. Oliver is an international writer, editor and consultant based in Devon. He is also the author of *A Footprint in the Sand*, an epic political comedy inspired by the end of the Cold War, and *The Anarchist's Arms*, a play set in near-future London.

In 2006, *The Bering Strait Crossing: A 21st century frontier* was published worldwide. In 2007, he was invited by the Russian Academy of Scientists to discuss the subject at the World Link conference in Moscow. By 2009, these materials had formed the basis for a Discovery Channel documentary on the theme. At the Shanghai World Expo 2010, the Beringia concept won the Grand Prix for innovation.

From 2007-2009, he lived in Paris on the Iĺe Saint Louis, where he also developed the original script for *The Pamphleteers*.

James Oliver is presently based at a remote location for his research on *Strait* of *Gibraltar: Non Plus Ultra - End of the World*.

He is a Fellow of the Royal Geographical Society.

For my shipmates in Paris,
and an unforgettable interlude (2007-2009)
on the Île Saint Louis under the
Single European Sky.

*"The power of the press is very great,
but not so great as the power to suppress."*

~ Lord Northcliffe
(Alfred Harmsworth).

Fashion before Ease (1793). The famous cartoon by
James Gilray depicts Tom Paine (a copy of _Rights of Man_
in his pocket) forcing a churlish Britannia into the
Constitution of her tight-fitting corset. (Earlier in his
unlikely career, Paine had been a staymaker.)
Courtesy: © Trustees of the British Museum.

Author's Note

The inspiration for this script is the author's business, as much as it is anyone's, but the passing reader may find some interest in its source. The original plan had been to write a profile of the short, curious, but highly productive career of Robert Greene (1558-1592): playmaker, pamphleteer, and chronicler of (and participant in) the 'low life' of Elizabethan London. Outside the scholarly realm, Greene has largely been forgotten, although the title of his Marlowesque play *Friar Bacon, Friar Bungay* remains familiar on the edge of memory. Even more obscurely, perhaps, he is also known as the pamphleteer behind *A Groatsworth of Wit Bought with a Million of Repentance* (1592): this is the tract that was found to contain a reference to an "upstart crowe"; that is, a provincial interloper in the London theatre world, which some scholars have taken as a rare allusion to the mysterious William Shakespeare.

There is more to Robert Greene than that, though: he is foremost among England's earliest working journalists. In the event, however, the plan to profile Greene was abandoned in favour of the present tract, since to study Greene is to evoke Thomas Nashe, among others. Poor Greene: another reincarnation is about to occur in these pages. After that, the wretched man will be left in peace as a select company of his fellow proto-journalists is profiled. As a special focus, the timeline aims to reveal how these early journalists were driven, not merely by scandal and sensationalism, but by major historical events on the world stage: the Reformation, the English Revolution, the intrigues of Queen Anne's reign in the War of the Spanish

Succession, the Seven Years' War, and the revolutions in America and in France.

The approach here, then, is to provide an overview of the span between Gutenberg and the French Revolution, and then to place profiles of seven pre-eminent pamphleteers on that same timeline.

In this way, the purpose of this brief excursion is to investigate the birth of journalism with the emergence of the periodical press as the 'fourth estate'.

James A. Oliver
Île Saint-Louis
Paris, 2009

CONTENTS

Illustrations &
TIMELINE

Overview

The Pamphleteers

Illustrations

Timeline
of *The Pamphleteers*

1439	Johannes Gutenberg conducts secret experiments with moveable type in Mainz, Germany.
1476	William Caxton establishes his press near Westminster Abbey.
1521·	Augustinian monk Martin Luther is excommunicated by Pope Leo X and outlawed by Emperor Charles V of the Holy Roman Empire.
	This act in effect triggers: the Reformation, the Counter Reformation, and the Thirty Years' War. In the war of propaganda, the phenomenon of pamphleteering emerges.
1549	*Requests for the Devonshyre and Cornyshe Rebelles* is a candidate for earliest 'news letter'.
1558	John Knox (co-founder of the Presbyterian Church in Scotland) lambasts the female monarchs of Europe with *The First Blast of the Trumpet Against the Monstrous Regiment of Women*. The broadside backfires when Mary Tudor's half-sister ascends the throne of England later that same year. Elizabeth I is not amused by Knox or his *Trumpet*.
1559	Elizabeth's advisers prepare the Injunctions of 1559 (based on Injunctions of Edward VI in 1547) · with Article LI for licensing of printed matter, *inc.* books, plays, and "infamous papers".
1580	Montaigne's *Essays* in French (translated into English 1603).

1583   The anti-Puritan John Whitgift is appointed Archbishop
            of Canterbury.

1584   The Puritans react with an anonymous pamphlet known
            as *A Learned Discourse*.

1586   Star Chamber powers invoked to control unlicensed
            printing.

1588-1590   Pamphleteering warfare breaks out with the Martin
            Prelate Controversy between Puritan fanatics and the
            established Church of England.

1590   *An Almond for a Parrot* (*attrib*. to Thomas Nashe).

1592   Robert Greene's *A Groatsworth of Wit Bought with a
            Million of Repentance* refers to a certain "upstart
            crowe" of the London theatre world, which some
            scholars have inferred as a rare allusion to William
            Shakespeare.

1592   Robert Greene's *A Quip for an Upstart Courtier* ridicules
            Gabriel Harvey. After the death of Greene, a pamphlet-
            eering feud breaks out between Harvey and Nashe.

1596   Thomas Nashe blasts the scholar Gabriel Harvey with
            the pamphlet *Have with You from Saffron Walden*.

1597   A counter-attack ensues with *The Trimming of
            Thomas Nashe, Gentleman*, probably by Richard
            Lichfield, a barber-surgeon of Cambridge, though the
            tract is often misattributed to the embittered Harvey.

1597   Francis Bacon publishes his early *Essays*.

1599   Thomas Nashe's final pamphlet *Nashe's Lenten Stuff*
            represents an early form of feature journalism far
            ahead of its time.

1599   The Bishops' Ban includes censure of Nashe and Harvey.

1603   The reign of James I commences.

1609   *The Gull's Horn Book* by Thomas Dekker is an eyewitness account of the Ordinaries (eating houses), theatres and taverns of London.

1618-1648   Thirty Years' War boosts demand for 'News' across Europe.

1621   Earliest (?) periodical in English arrives in London from Amsterdam: the *Corante* reports weekly (under licence) on news from Europe.

1631   In France, Cardinal Richelieu is behind the launch of the *Gazette* for news and propaganda.

1637   Star Chamber decree stipulates that the author's name is identified on all publications, but not every printer conforms.

1642-51   English Civil Wars [1642-1646; 1648-1649; 1649-1651]

1641   The Long Parliament (1640-1660) abolishes the Star Chamber. The subsequent eruption of unlicensed printing provokes the Stationers' Company to petition Parliament for control of the press.

1642   Theatres are closed by decree.

1643   Parliament enacts the Printing Ordinance to control unlicensed printing.

1643-46   The emergence of weekly 'News Books' with Marchmont Nedham's anti-Royalist *Mercurius Britanicus*. Nedham is jailed.

1644   John Milton's pamphlet *Areopagitica* is named for a
            hill in Athens. In the form of a speech to Parliament,
            the tract is Milton's response to the 1643 Ordinance
            by way of a plea for freedom of thought.

1647-49   On his release, Nedham changes sides with the pro-
            Royalist weekly *Mercurius Pragmaticus*. Nedham is
            jailed again when the Parliamentarians seize power.

            A group of Republican activists, The Levellers
            promote tax and voting reform, and an end to the
            class system. Accused of conspiracy, the Levellers are
            crushed by Cromwell's troops.

1649   Charles I is executed.

1649-1659   Interregnum of the Commonwealth. The governing
            Council of State (1649-1653) is superseded by the
            Office of Lord Protector held by Oliver Cromwell
            (1653-1658) and Richard Cromwell (1658-1659).

            In this decade, Marchmont Nedham changes sides yet
            again and publishes the *Mercurius Politicus* in
            support of the Commonwealth.

1660   The Restoration with Charles II.

            Marchmont Nedham flees England for the Continent.

            As a prominent figure in the outgoing regime, John
            Milton narrowly escapes the gallows.

1662   The Printing Act.
            Pamphleteering enters a period of decline.

1665   *The Oxford Gazette* is established as the bi-weekly
            official 'newspaper' of government.

The Royal Society's *Philosophical Transactions* is the world's first scientific journal.

1666   *Oxford Gazette* is renamed the *London Gazette*.

1685   James II crushes the Monmouth Rebellion at the Battle of Sedgemore. Daniel Defoe probably takes part - on the losing side. A general pardon includes the fugitive Defoe.

1688   Overthrow of James II. The Glorious Revolution: William of Orange is installed on the throne of England as William III with Mary Stuart as Queen.

1690   Jacobite forces (*i.e.,* loyal to James II) defeated at the Battle of the Boyne.

1695   Print Act (1662; extended 1679) final expiration. In the next decade, relaxation of censorship opens the way for the early periodical press in the reign of Queen Anne.

1701   Defoe's satirical verse pamphlet *True-Born Englishman* defends William III against those who see a 'foreigner' on the throne of England.

1701-1714   War of the Spanish Succession

1702   Reign of Queen Anne inaugurated.

            The Daily Courant is England's first *daily* periodical, based in Fleet Street, London

1703   Daniel Defoe's *The Shortest War with Dissenters*.

1704-1713   The *Review* "News Paper" is published by Daniel Defoe, with the support of Robert Harley, First Minister to Queen Anne.

At home, the *Review* promotes government policy for the Act of Union of Scotland and England. Abroad, the paper supports the Duke of Marlborough's Mediterranean campaign.

1707   Act of Union of Scotland and England.

1708-10   Robert Harley is forced out of office; by 1710 he has defected to the Tories.

1709-1712   Joseph Addison and Richard Steele produce *The Tatler* (1709-11) succeeded by *The Spectator* (1711-12).

1710-11   Jonathan Swift edits the moderate, Tory-aligned *The Examiner.*

1711   Robert Harley regains office with the incoming Tory Ministry. Swift's *Conduct of the Allies* promotes a Tory manifesto to end the war in Europe. Queen Anne dismisses Marlborough.

1713-14   Treaty of Utrecht (1713) extricates England from the War of Spanish Succession, which concludes with the Treaty of the Rastatt (1714).

              The reign of George I (1714-27) commences.

1729   Jonathan Swift's satirical pamphlet *A Modest Proposal* ridicules the land-owning classes in Ireland.

1724-25   As "M.B. Drapier", Dean Swift's cycle of pamphlets *The Drapier's Letters* attacks the British government's plan to introduce an inferior currency for use in Ireland. The scheme is discredited, and Robert Walpole is forced to withdraw the patent.

1756-73   The Seven Years' War.

1775-1783   American War of Independence.

1776   Tom Paine publishes *Common Sense* with the byline
             "Written by an Englishman" in which he makes the
             case for American independence from Britain.

1789-99   The French Revolution and the 'Reign of Terror'.

1790   British statesman Edmund Burke's *Reflections on the
             French Revolution.*

             In this same year, Mary Wollstonecraft responds with
             Vindication of the Rights of Men.

1791-92   In *Rights of Man*, Paine defends the French
             Revolution against the denunciations of Burke.

             Mary Wollstonecraft's revolutionary *A Vindication of
             the Rights of Woman* (1792).

1794-95   Tom Paine's *The Age of Reason*. An Enlightenment
             perspective on the biblical account, Paine is vilified as
             an atheist and a drunkard.

1809   Tom Paine dies at Greenwich Village, New York. A
             burial on consecrated ground refused, he is interred at
             his La Rochelle farm.

             *In 1948, the people of Paris erected a gold-plated
             statue of Paine at the Parc Montsouris by the Cité
             Universitaire:*

             Citoyen du Monde - "Citizen of the World".

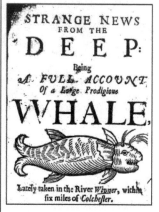

Fig.1~Fig 4. Early Pamphlets (*clockwise*): *Discovery of a Witch* (1643); *Life and Death of Gamaliell Ratsey* (1605), a notorious highwayman; *Strange News from the Deep* (1677) reports on a whale beached on the Essex coast; *Comet* (1596) sighted over Germany.

Overview

Origins and Themes

THE WORD pamphlet has its roots with a form of Latin love poem, popular in the twelfth century: *Pamphilus, seu de Amore*, later foreshortened to Pamphilet, which is thought to derive from Pan as the Greek god of the pasture (*paein*), a chaser of nymphs. The pamphlet, then, served as the agency of transmission for such passion in the form of verse.

In the great age of pamphleteering, though, there was not much in the way of love poetry on offer. The terms *Blast* and *Broadside* are repeatedly associated with the *vituperative* nature of the form, as are *Trumpet* and even *Bugle*. In such soundings-off, the pamphlet form tended to be viewed as an instrument of anti-establishmentarian subversives, or as a source of unreliable or biased news. There was always the risk, too, that the pamphlet, as with some old blunderbuss, might explode in its author's face, such that these same subversives might identify themselves.

In the early days, the pamphlet offered an outlet for eccentrics, religious fanatics, and those with an agenda of vested interest - as well as printers in search of fast profits. The early pamphleteers explored overarching themes with a form of sensationalist journalism not so far removed from the obsessions of today: plague, witchcraft, reports from distant lands where unlikely creatures were said to exist, dire warnings, rebellions and uprisings, atrocities, dubious reportage on strange happenings, bizarre weather phenomena, and revelation as a pioneering kind of 'news' reportage in times of crisis (*see Figs. 1~4*).

The pamphlet form also provided a ready-made paper platform or missile for heated disputation, the unmasking of hypocrites, diatribe, spat and counter-spat, long-running religious controversy, secular satire in the cause of social reform, and even revolutionary manifesto.

As the form evolved, then so political elites and governments were to learn the ways of the pamphleteer as a powerful means of propaganda.

Gutenberg and Caxton

A timeline for the pamphleteering phenomenon is established with events spanned by the innovations of the Renaissance, the upheavals of the Reformation, and the Revolutions in American and in France: there, to reach the high-water mark with Tom Paine (1737-1809) and Mary Wollstonecraft (1759-1797). After this interval, the importance of the pamphlet is eclipsed with the emergence and explosive growth of the periodical press.

The revolution-in-print originated in Germany with Johannes Gutenberg (c.1400 - c.1468), who made the breakthrough that changed the face of print and of the civilized world. As early as 1439, documentary evidence reveals that Gutenberg had been engaged with secret experiments involving moveable metallic type. By 1455, he was based in Mainz with a partner, Johann Fust, a moneylender.[1] In any event, printer and financier went their separate ways, but not before Fust had seized Gutenberg's equipment, since, most likely, his associate had defaulted on an inflexible loan. In this way, also by

---

[1] The world-famous Gutenberg Bible or Mazarin Bible is thought to have originated from this same press. The book was rediscovered c. 1760 at Cardinal Mazarin's residence in Paris.

default, Fust continued with the printing business. The centuries of monks copying-out books by hand eventually came to an end, which would diminish the influence and power of the monasteries. The Gutenberg-Fust alliance had developed this innovative print technology, which came to spawn a global industry.

OUT OF ENGLAND, William Caxton (*c.* 1422 - *c.* 1491) operated as a merchant of textiles (a trade pre-allied with printing) with interests in the Netherlands, where in Bruges he encountered the miracle of metallic type. There was, though, much more to Caxton than textile and print: he also proved himself an outstanding translator. Whatever Caxton translated got printed, and whatever he translated came to be the first ever printed works in the English language. For his inaugural project, Caxton turned to ancient myth. By 1474-75, he had already embarked on the formidable task of a translation, from the French, of *Recuyell of the Histories' of Troy*, which became the first book to appear in English, and not, as is often presupposed, The Bible, which would no doubt have presented certain difficulties. So, Caxton, who was still in Bruges at this time, had printed the first book in English outside of England on a very un-English subject.

The year 1476 marked Caxton's return to London, where he established his famous press in the vicinity of Westminster Abbey. From that strategic locale, over eighty books flowed from the press, with Geoffrey Chaucer's *Canterbury Tales* (*orig. c.* 1387-1400) as the first book published by Caxton on English soil, and including Sir Edmund Malory's *Mort d'Arthur* (1485) - to unleash a cultural transformation across the land.

FOR THE FIRST time, the work of remote and obscure scribes had been harnessed and then multiplied by the new machinery. In the immediate wake of the Gutenberg revolution in print, there was no such entity as a printed pamphlet, and anyway the new technology was reserved for works of high literary seriousness translated from the languages of antiquity: histories, philosophical treatises epic poems, & etc.

If big, leafy books on ancient themes could be printed or 'published', then so might shorter books, not even books, but slim, unbound books or *pamphlets*. . .and in English.

Pamphlet or Essay?

By the time of Caxton, the old Anglo-Saxon had emerged as Middle English marked by the influences of Latin and French (as the official language in England after the Norman Conquest). The speaker and reader of this common or vulgar tongue gradually converged on the printed page, and for which printers craved rules and standardization. Those who could not read, which was most people, could be *read to* as a much wider *audience* - being those who *listen*. For both reader and listener, the very sight of a pamphlet would have been a cause of fascination - and suspicion.

As the influence of written English spread, there were those scholars and diplomats who for long after clung onto Latin versions of their well-honed texts as the preferred or elevated mode of expression. In this way, Francis Bacon - lawyer, scientist, philosopher, Queen's Counsel in the prosecution of the Earl of Essex - developed both Latin and English as a scientific language with his early *Essays* (1597). Bacon's main influence had been the real pioneer of the *essai* (Fr.=trial), Michel de Montaigne (1533-1592), whose works were eventually published in 1580 and translated into English in 1603. These high-minded thinkers, though, were not obscure pamphleteers, but aristocrats (and a lawyer) with philosophical inclinations as essayists and men of ideas whose footprints are permanent. Philosophers are not proto-journalists, and *vice versa*, though ideally both could be said to be seekers of some truth or version of the truth, being a kind of reportage from the front-line, while the pamphleteers strayed into wayward sensationalism as an early form of agitprop (=agitation propaganda) - or to achieve sales.

In Europe, then, the timeline shows that the efforts of the earliest pamphleteers - John Knox, *et al* - predate the essayists - Montaigne, Bacon, Abraham Cowley, *et. al.* - whose output was eventually collected in book-form; these are not shoddy pamphlets. Essays are not 'hackwork', with the priority on erudite investigation or enquiry, and tend not to propagandise any cause or version of the truth, although exceptions occurred when the search for reality, say, was interpreted as scientific heresy; whereas the pamphlet form might have been seen, on occasion, to point in the direction of low or even high treason.

There is an illusion of essay and pamphlet co-evolving; but this is not really the case, and a twilight area exists between printed pamphlet, printed speeches (as with the *Arcopagitica* of Milton), scientific treatises such as those of Galilei Galileo and John Dee, very short books, very long pamphlets, and so on. In expressly physical form, the pamphlet is a term typically used to connote a short, unbound publication without hard covers, and likely privately printed - that is, in a later era, *samizdat*.[1]

---

[1] From the Russian for 'self-publication' of unauthorized texts.

The pamphlet, too, is usually set apart (from the essay) as a paper missile or broadside in the war of words, with the possibility that a forked tongue might reside very firmly inside its cheek. There are, of course, those cases where an essay might be published as a pamphlet; but then again the essay is the tool of thinkers, and pamphleteers and journalists are usually not big thinkers. Either way, things become entangled. For clarity, the timeline indicates that the *essay* form post-dates the pamphlet and generally retains the high ground to this day. As for intentions: P is for Propaganda, where E is for Enquiry.

Schism and Reformation

The timeline reveals that by the early sixteenth century powerful socio-political and religious currents coursed through Europe with deeply enmeshed geopolitical dimensions that drove the machinery of the printing press.

Geographers will note that, whereas the Great Schism of 1058 divided the Church between eastern (Constantinople) and western (Rome), then so the Reformation split that 'west' between north and south. In 1521, the Roman Catholic Church fell into a chasm over Pope Leo X's excommunication of Martin Luther (1483-1546), the campaigning Augustinian monk of Wittenberg. Then, following the Diet of Worms[1], Emperor Charles V of the Holy Roman Empire[2] placed Luther under a ban.

---

[1] The town of Worms is on the Rhine.
[2] The Holy Roman Empire (800/962~1806) was the fusion of central European states - variously, of Germany, Italy and Burgundy - "neither Holy, Roman, nor an Empire" according to one historian with a ready wit. The Diet referred to the general assembly of its constituent states.

The Diet of Worms was well named: a tidal wave of religious conflict swept across Europe, with the Reformation, the Counter-Reformation, and - eventually - the Thirty Years' War (1618-1648) - a period of upheaval that created great demand for 'News' of foreign affairs throughout Europe. The era of pamphleteering warfare essentially arrived with the onset of the Reformation. In the battle of ideas, the phenomenon of pamphleteering, with the technology of 'the press' already established, was forged.

In Britain, among the earliest of these pamphleteers was John Knox (1510-1572), who spoke and wrote with early approval of the Lutheran vision, and himself became founder (with John Calvin's support) of the Presbyterian Church in Scotland. Beyond an excessively bold attack on the Emperor, Knox's most infamous pamphlet is a high-level exercise in misogyny: *The First Blast of the Trumpet Against the Monstrous Regiment of Women* (1558), an ill-advised assault on female monarchs, with Mary Tudor primarily in his sights. When Mary Tudor's half-sister ascended the throne of England that same year as Elizabeth I, the new Queen had Knox in *her* sights. A woman monarch, scorned? Knox surely had not known what he was in for; and although he had intended no such offence to that especial prince, his *Trumpet* promptly misfired. This is an early example of a pamphlet exploding in its author's face with unintended consequences. John Knox, who might have played a significant role in the English Reformation, was kept in his Caledonian box.

Infamous Papers

The year after the *Trumpet*, Elizabeth's Privy Council advisers prepared the Injunctions of 1559 (based on the

Injunctions of Edward VI in 1547) · *inc.* Article LI for the
licensing of printed matter, such as books, plays, and
"infamous papers", which thenceforth might be interpreted as seditious fulminations against the State.

In the long reign of Elizabeth, such 'infamous papers'
surfaced in respect of certain high-profile *cause célèbre*. In
the case of Jesuit priest Edmund Campion, whom the
Queen held in high esteem, he had challenged the *status
quo* with his *Decem Rationes* or *Ten Reasons* (against the
Church of England). In 1580, the fugitive Campion was
hunted down, questioned, tortured, and sent to the block
on 1 December 1581. In the most notorious case of the
Robert Devereux, the second Earl of Essex (1565-1601),
the expensively printed *First Year of King Henry the
Fourth* was considered by the Queen and some of her
advisors as a "seditious prelude to put into the people's
heads".[1] The (otherwise anonymous) tract had been
dedicated to Essex. After a spectacular trial, with the
prosecution team headed by Attorney General Sir Edward
Coke, Essex was found guilty of high treason, and went to
the block on 25 February 1601. In her own way, of course,
Elizabeth was heartbroken.

Robert Greene, Thomas Nashe, and the Early Journalism

Robert Greene (1558-1592) perhaps came closest to the
original meaning and intent of *pamphilus, seu de Amore*
with his 'romances', but he soon turned to very different
subject matter with such tracts as *A Groatsworth of Wit
Bought with a Million of Repentance* (1592) in which he

---

[1] Refer: *Sir Francis Bacon His Apology in Certain Imputations
Concerning the late Earl of Essex* (1604).

warns his readers against the dangers of dissipation with dark insights of the Elizabethan London underworld. Robert Greene and Thomas Nashe (1567-1601?) were among England's earliest 'journalists'. There are, of course, earlier instances of newssheets by obscure reporters across Renaissance Europe, notably in Venice (1551) and Cologne (1594) and London (1592) {see Emergence of the Press}, but for now the focus remains with the pamphleteers as early journalists. The term, which derives from the Old French *jurnal* for daily record, was not in common usage until a much later era. A day's travel is a journey, and a day's record is a journal. For this era, the term and function 'reporter' is apt (Latin= *reportare*='to bring back'), but also unfamiliar then, although this stalks after 'intelligencer' of the kind employed by Francis Walsingham. This, though, delves into a clandestine world where information is collected, and not broadcast, unless for the purposes of disinformation as distraction.

The byline pamphlets of Greene and Nashe, on the other hand, are cast in an open and sometimes direct way, and derived from actual, *lived* experience. This approach had been a long time in the making; and, although the likes of a Watergate scandal that toppled a president lay far into the future, the pamphleteers of the 1590s were the original investigative journalists, and often as inflammatory.

The Marprelate Controversy

In times of ideological conflicts, these early journalists found themselves courted by paymasters, such as plutocratic, high church clergy eager to counter the fallout from the highly combustible Martin Prelate or

Marprelate Controversy. The Reformation in England, with the split from Rome, led to the establishment of the Church of England, which had soon alienated the puritanical fringe. This was a battle between those who wanted any taint of Popery erased (the Puritans) and those who were observed by some as clinging too closely to the old ways (the high church clergy). The protracted cycle of pamphlets (1588-90) represents the conflict between the mysterious "Martin" on the side of the fanatical puritans and those anonymous writers on the establishment side, such as Nashe and Greene, who were clearly inspired by "Martin's" eccentric style. The cycle of pamphlets seems to reach a conclusion with *An Almond for a Parrot* (1590), which has been attributed to Nashe.

Reprisals, often vicious, marked the end of the affair: the secret printing press of the Marprelates was located, and the printer, a Mr John Penry, escaped to Scotland, but was later captured and executed in 1593. The real author (or authors) behind 'Martin' escaped, identity cloaked, though suspicion would appear to have fallen on a certain Job Throckmorton, a gentleman of War-wickshire. There were many others suspected of association with the secret presses one way or another; those who were eventually tracked down by the Stationers' Company were fined and imprisoned.

The pamphlets on "Martin's" side were written in an easy style (*i.e.,* puritan; unadorned), which had not hitherto been seen in England - or anywhere else. Thomas Nashe, who outlived Greene, was the main exponent of the anonymous "Martin's" easy, witty prose style - a fustian word is *trenchant* - since Nashe himself had been the primary seeker of what he called the "extemporal vein" (that is, 'off-the-cuff') for English reportage. As a result,

Nashe turned himself into a kind of feature journalist (the stuff of today's Sunday colour supplements); he was way ahead of his time with such as *Nashe's Lenten Stuff* (1599), a highly eccentric evocation of the Great Yarmouth herring industry. This is Nashe's final outing as a pamphleteer, and the birth of feature journalism.

Interlude

An interlude is provided (before returning to the fanatical Puritans) in the company of the good-natured, happy-go-lucky Thomas Dekker (1572?-1632). Alongside Nashe and Greene, Dekker is exceptional in that, unlike those playwrights · Shakespeare, Marlowe, et. al · who did not leave much, or any, trace in prose, he engaged in the work of pamphlets as well as plays. The most noteworthy (for its realism) among his plays is *The Shoemaker's Holiday* (1599), which, according to Philip Henslowe's diary for the Fortune Theatre, was performed before the Court. When the theatres were ordered closed in time of plague, Dekker must have sought diversion, and no doubt The Mermaid Tavern, of which he was likely a regular, provided a refuge. The outbreaks also supplied Dekker with fodder for plague pamphlets, a well-ploughed furrow or theme for the early pamphleteers, and of which he wrote several.

In *The Gull's Horn Book* (1609), there is evidence for a great pamphleteer in his prime. This pamphlet remains outstanding as a valuable social document, an eyewitness account of London life in the locus of Dekker's daily routine from the Ordinary (eating house), then to the theatre, and onward for the tavern, there to rub shoulders with the playmakers, poets, and gallants of the day.

The English Revolution

The passing of Elizabeth I in 1603 brought the Tudor dynasty to an end. The House of Stuart assumed pre-eminence with the reign of James I (1603-1625). In the reign of Charles I (1625-1649), the fanatical Puritans eventually got their way, although the clash was essentially over Parliament's ability to raise money, which had to be paid for with much blood through the hell-fire confrontations of the English Civil War. Pamphleteering warfare on an unprecedented scale reflected the military clashes between Parliamentarian forces and those of the Royalists. Along with this massive flurry of pamphlets, the 'News Book' appeared at this time, too, with the strange case of the editor Marchmont Nedham (1620-1678), who aligned himself with both sides during the hostilities, although not at the same time. The weekly *Mercurius Britannicus* (1643-46) attacked the Royalists, for which Nedham was jailed on charges of sedition. On his release, he launched the Royalist weekly *Mercurius Pragmaticus* (1647-49). When the Parliamentarians came to power, Nedham was again sent to prison. On his re-release, he produced *Mercurius Politicus* (1650-60) in support of the Commonwealth.

In the minds of the Puritans, the Reformation had reached completion with the execution of Charles I and the English Revolution of 1649. In the aftermath, the Commonwealth · retrospectively, the Interregnum · covered the period to the Restoration with Charles II in 1660.

By far the most famous pamphleteer of this era is John Milton (1608-1674), who flourished in the highly-charged atmosphere of the Interregnum. The great poems came much later. As a young writer, he focused on divorce pamphlets, which were intended as an exercise in self-promotion. The lofty-minded Milton found himself (with his knowledge of classical languages) appointed as Secretary of Foreign Tongues or Latin Secretary of the Commonwealth. In this role, Milton acted as chief propagandist-apologist for the Cromwell regime to placate nervous allies in Europe (appalled by the removal of Charles I), and who remained agitated as to the possible intentions of the new order as to the near abroad. John Milton excelled in this role, with perhaps too high a profile. By the time of Restoration, he narrowly survived the gallows, and so lived to dictate *Paradise Lost* in blind old age.

As a pamphleteer, John Milton's high achievement is the *Areopagitica* (1644), named for a hill in Athens. The pamphlet is Milton's view of unlicensed printing *versus* censorship, that is, the freedom of the press.

The Star Chamber and Censorship

The Star Chamber had originated with Henry VII in 1487 as a legal instrument by which to control the nobility (and so named for a star-shaped symbol on the ceiling of that court room at the Palace of Westminster). By 1586, the bishops of London had reclaimed the powers of the Star Chamber. In the reign of the Stuarts, the Chamber had become the device of royal sanction. As an exercise in arbitrary power, the Court of judges had been notorious as an agency of interrogation, imprisonment, torture and execution. In 1641, the Long Parliament abolished the Star Chamber Court of Charles I, which unleashed a wave of unlicensed printing; this provoked the Stationer's Company to petition Parliament for a reinforcement of its charter monopoly for control of the press.

The House responded with the enactment of the Printing Ordinance of 1643. The *Areopagitica* is Milton's response in the form of a notional speech to Parliament. *Areopagitica* is the very antithesis of propaganda, and clearly argues, based on ancient precedent, the case for free expression, which, for Milton, meant freedom of thought. The pamphlet had come of age.

The Levellers

The pamphlets of sixteenth and seventeenth century were renowned for their extended, quaint, bizarre, or enigmatic titles. The titles alone (which embedded the entire theme of what was on offer) were often superior to the content. The title was a headline, a come-on, a tease, and surely an invitation to purchase. Pan, then, is still chasing his nymphs in the pasture. The text of the pamphlet might even live up to what was on offer, but more often this was thin gruel indeed. There are those outstanding exceptions, where the material matched or exceeded the expectations stimulated by the title, such that some higher purpose might be served.

The enigmatic *Light Shining Over Buckinghamshire* (1648) reveals a manifesto extraordinarily prescient for its day in terms of what would now be called 'democratic rights'. But what might this light be that shines over that garden county? The subtitle of the anonymous pamphlet reveals its intention: *A Discovery of the main ground, original Cause of all the Slavery in the world, but chiefly in England: presented by way of a Declaration of many of the well affected in that County, to all their poore oppressed Country men of England, &c.*

This anonymous tract has the look of (and about the right date for) a Leveller pamphlet.

The Levellers (1647-49) were a short-lived group of Republican activists and pamphleteers led by John Lilburn (1614?-57) and Sir Richard Overton (1625-1664). As their name suggests, they sought an end to the class structure, with wide-scale voting and tax reforms; that is, until the Levellers - caught up in some conspiracy to overthrow the government - were themselves levelled by Cromwell's thugs. So that was the end for the Levellers; and, for the Commonwealth, too, the end was near.

Restoration and Emergence of the Press

After the Restoration of 1660, with Charles II installed on the throne of England, the war of propaganda had been fought. Thereafter, with the advent of the Printing Act of 1662 to reassert the royal prerogative, the pamphlet form entered a period of relative decline. The immediate consequences were a revival of manuscript, and - to some extent - unlicensed printing. By 1665, the government had established the weekly *Oxford Gazette* (renamed the London Gazette in 1666), while the Court of Charles II was in retreat in that city, as the 'official news paper'. In this way, the government had effectively reached out and claimed a virtual monopoly over 'the press'.

The origin of the term *gazette* is intriguing. The word is taken from the Venetian *gazeta de la novità* - or 'a half-penny worth of news'- a manuscript 'news sheet' first published in about 1556 and circulated by the city-state throughout southern Europe. In France, as long ago as 1631, Cardinal Richelieu had established the weekly *Gazette* as an instrument of news and propaganda. There are, of course, precedents for the printed (as opposed to manuscript) 'news paper' elsewhere in Europe, with

periodicals recognisable as 'news papers' appearing in
Strasbourg by 1605, Augsburgh in Germany by 1609, and
Amsterdam (the first anywhere in English) by 1618-1620.
In Asia, where print technology had originated in Korea
and China, the *Peking Gazette* made the great leap
forward with the changeover from woodblock to moveable
type in 1638.

The case for the *earliest* title is uncertain. A candidate
for precedence by way of a 'news letter' is *Requests for the
Devonshyre and Corniche Rebelles* (1549). In Europe, the
Mercurius Gallobelgicus out of Cologne made its debut in
1594 and *News out of France* appears as early 1592. Based
in England, the earliest news periodical would appear to
be the *Corante* in about 1621, with weekly coverage
(translated into English under licence) of news from
Europe, and published by the mysterious "NB". There
followed many such 'corantos' (licences to print). On the
scientific front, the Royal Society introduced *Philosophical Transactions* in 1665, the first journal of its kind
anywhere in the world; while, from the sublime to the
mundane, John Dunton's weekly *Athenian Mercury* (1691-
7) supplied the prototype of the format for Readers'
Questions and Answers.

In 1690, across the Atlantic, the first attempt at a 'news
paper' for the American colonies was the Boston-based
Publick Occurrences both Forreign and Domestick.
Although launched as a periodical, the title was supp-
ressed on charges of sedition after a single issue. In 1704,
the *Boston Newsletter* proved more successful and is
recognised as the first American periodical.

In Britain again, the periodical press of this era had
emerged with the relaxation of censorship (final expiration
of the Printing Act 1694-95), and the explosive growth of

coffee houses as the 'news rooms' of London. As the reign of King William III gave way to Queen Anne (1702-1714), the intrigues of the Whigs and Tories inaugurated the era of the partisan press, either along party political lines or indeed with the various expressions of the Opposition press. In 1702, the neutral *Daily Courant* appeared as England's first *daily* 'news paper'. Established in rooms located conveniently above the White Hart Inn on Fleet Street, the paper was among those early pioneers of a worldwide revolution in the press that would one day become synonymous with that street in London EC4.

Satire

By the early years of the eighteenth century, the pamphleteers were employing satire of a vicious or excruciating nature, even at a sophisticated or sublime level. The etymology is obscure. In the Latin *Satis= enough*. From the Greek, a satyr is a companion of Pan or Dionysus, and a Satyr Play was a light-hearted follow-up to the main acts (extant in Euripides' *Cyclops*). In *Discourse on Satire* (1690), John Dryden traced the origins of satire as from the Latin "sature", *i.e.*, sated or enough, or *satura* - a medley, full of variety. Both of these definitions seem to satisfy the conditions, although the Latin root now tends to be accepted over the Greek *satyr* as proposed by the Italian scholar Joseph Scaliger.

Either way, there were those outsiders or non-conformists who were unable to resist aiming the pamphlet-missile to blast the establishment. In this way, Daniel Defoe (1660?-1731) serves as a case study for a satire that exploded in its author's face. The licensing of pamphlets had been permitted to lapse back in 1685, but this did not imply that the establishment was prepared to invite or tolerate ridicule. *The Shortest Way with Dissenters* (1703) proposed that non-conformists (*i.e.*, those Protestants who stood apart from the established Church of England) should be summarily despatched. There were whispers in high church circles among those inclined to agree; that is, until they discovered that Defoe was himself a non-conformist, and that the tract was · wasn't it? · a skit? The reaction of the authorities (stung by the ridicule) was severe: Defoe was fined, sent to the pillory, and imprisoned. On his release, he was a changed man, with a long career as propagandist that stretched out ahead of the future author of *Robinson Crusoe.*

In this era, Jonathan Swift, Dean of St. Patrick's in Dublin, author of *Tale of a Tub* (1704) and *Gulliver's Travels* (1726), is the usual suspect for one of the most notorious pamphlets ever produced. If *A Modest Proposal* (1729) is high irony or satire, not everyone could be counted on to see the tract in quite that way. The subject matter (albeit not the specific solution) is revealed with the complete title... *for Preventing the Poor People in Ireland from being a Burden to their Parents or the Country; and for making them beneficial to the Publick.* The "proposal" of the title?: that the poor should sell their babies to the rich as a source of food. There were those among the reading public, no doubt, who took Swift · a clergyman bachelor · at his word. The idea that the tract might be a satirical shock-tactic passed over many heads; among the gentry, the tract was considered as "in poor taste" · a judgement basted with unintended irony. This is the Dean's real target: the wealthy landlords, who appeared quite indifferent to the human squalor and degradations surrounding their grand estates. The pamphlet, supported by deadly relevant statistics, is generally regarded as a masterpiece of sustained ironical narrative. *A Modest Proposal* makes for grizzly reading even today.

A complex character often accused of misanthropy, Swift sought preferment in the Church, while undermining his own strategy with the stance of ridiculing society. Interestingly, he did not laugh (according to his biographers), either in public or in private. Instead, he presented the same steady mask to the world. In the end, he lost his mind, but at a respectable old age; and, before doing so, he willed the bulk of his fortune to found a lunatic asylum in Dublin.

Propaganda and the Early Press

The early eighteenth century in the reign of Queen Anne is the interval where the overlap occurs with pamphleteering and the emergent periodical journalism. In the hands of vested interest (usually the Whigs or the Tories), 'hacks' were hired for demolishing the policies of the Opposition (if they had any), and so pamphlet and periodical were powerful ways of directing public opinion by way of propaganda. Daniel Defoe, sprung from jail, was ahead of the game with his *Review* (1704-1713).

For this very special project, he had on this occasion a powerful patron (the government) under the cloaked auspices of a senior cabinet minister: Robert Harley, who at various times in the political cycle patronised both Defoe and the rival Swift. Defoe's one-man production (he is the inventor of the bogus Letter to the Editor) of the *Review* remarked on developments in the War of the Spanish Succession (1701-1714), and promoted the government's policy in that direction. As Defoe remarked, his "News Paper" was like "writing history by inches". As a non-conformist and denizen of Grub Street, Defoe was an outsider; even so, jealous eyes more clubbable regarded his efforts with great interest, since careers might in this way be advanced. Soon enough, and clearly modelled after the *Review*, Joseph Addison and Richard Steele launched *The Tatler* (1709-11) succeeded by *The Spectator* (1711-12) - both titles were, in good time, revived in a later era.

Swift contributed to both these periodicals, and so came to be admired for his highly effective prose and sharp wit. From the side-lines of social exclusion, Defoe lampooned his great rival for writing polite 'tittle-tattle' of no consequence while moving in the elevated circles of society and knowing how to "sit at the right tables". As for Defoe, he was never invited to such convivial tables. Robert Harley, who had found a special mission for the remarkable outsider Daniel Defoe, now turned to the sophisticated Swift for high-level propaganda: with articles for the moderate Tory *Examiner* (1710); and the pamphlet *Conduct of the Allies* (1711), which promoted a peace deal ahead of the Treaty of Utrecht (1713). For a time First Minister to Queen Anne, Harley is among the earliest of politicians to seize on the potential of journalism as propaganda over censorship, and in this way he cultivated both Defoe and Swift for intrigue at an international level.

Enlightenment and Revolution

The Enlightenment is generally considered by historians as the span of the eighteenth century when ideas were being considered through reason and philosophical enquiry instead of the accepted norms of tradition. As such, this is a time of revolution in America and in Europe, when the established structures of society are being replaced through innovation in science, politics, and government. In this era, the zenith of the age of the pamphleteers is well represented by Tom Paine (1737-1809). The beginnings were not encouraging for the man who would eventually produce *Rights of Man* (1791-92). For Tom Paine, born of Thetford in Norfolk, the journey from stay-maker to excise man, then revolutionary journalist, makes for a highly improbable case history in the chronicles of the pamphleteers. As an excise man, Paine's first outing as pamphleteer was *The Case for Excise Officers* (1772), which incurred his dismissal from the service.

In late 1774, he travelled to America, where he found employment as the managing editor of the *Pennsylvania Magazine.*

Tom Paine achieved great fame in the colonies with his forty-eight-page *Common Sense,* which made the case, with perfect timing (10 January 1776), for American independence from Britain. The byline "Written by an Englishman" concealed his identity, since the views expressed were high treason in the eyes of England.

For the main title of the pamphlet, Paine abandoned the tradition of the quaint, bizarre and the enigmatic; and, although *Common Sense* considers a great theme, the title indicates no such epic quality or dramatic perspective. Then again, there is such a quality as the power of understatement. The pamphlet sold 500,000 copies in its first year. The famous sentence: "There is something very absurd in supposing a Continent to be perpetually governed by an island," forms part of Paine's case for the break with England. In the greater sphere, *Common Sense* is considered to have shaped the *American Declaration of Independence.*

There are, however, primary influences at work here in the shape of John Locke (1632-1704) and Montesquieu (1689-1755). The *Declaration,* then, with *Magna Carta* as a distant antecedent, reveals the fingerprints of the English philosopher and the French political thinker on the separation of powers as much as anyone else's.

By this time, war had broken out between Britain and the colonies. In this period, Paine produced a series of pamphlets collected as *American Crisis* (1776-83). In *Public Good* (1780), for instance, he argued for union among the former colonies, with an early vision for a "United States".

In 1787, he travelled to England and France, and along the way he became embroiled in the French Revolution. In *Rights of Man*, Paine rebuked the English statesman Edmund Burke (1729-1797), who had condemned the French Revolution. In her own special way, though, Mary Wollstonecraft (1759-1797) had pre-empted Paine with her pamphlet *A Vindication of the Rights of Men* (1790) with very similar reflections as *Rights of Man.* In 1792, she went on to publish *Vindication of the Rights of Woman* in which she challenged the rigid pre-conceptions of the society in which she lived. As for Tom Paine, he ended his days as a man reviled, his reputation destroyed. In *The Age of Reason* (1794-95), he made a close study of The Bible for consistency in terms of a documentary account. If *Common Sense* had been treasonous in British eyes, then there were those who saw *The Age of Reason* as nothing less than sacrilegious. In 1809, Paine died in debauched circumstances. A church burial refused, his body was interred at his New Rochelle farm. In 1819, his remains were shipped to England, but his bones went missing on the voyage.

The body of work, unlike the bones, endures.

A great deal of Tom Paine's journalism might have been serialized in the press, with some obvious exceptions, but he chose the extended pamphlet-form instead, and so this brings the timeline to an end.

BEYOND THE timeframe considered, the pamphlet form was revived many times in the nineteenth and twentieth century, but instances of "infamous papers" become rare in the age of the periodical press. As an instance, Émile Zola's infamous *J'Accus..!* was published, not as a pamphlet, but as a front-page newspaper article in *L'Aurore* on 13 January 1898. In the age of organised propaganda, saturation television coverage, disinformation, news entertainment, public relations, the libel laws, lobbyists, the *spinmeister*, and the 'open sewer' of the internet, the role of the pamphlet has been eclipsed.[1] The authorities have never had it so good, since the public do not know what to believe in an ocean of disinformation. An impression prevails that modern pamphleteers do not have much, or anything, to say; while the politicians of today appear to be more than capable of lampooning themselves.

The pamphlet form remains (intriguingly) as an open channel for subverting or bypassing the establishment press, either in print or the digital equivalent, but again its role in the era of the mass media is diminished to the point where these efforts coalesce into the 'great unread'. In the present era, though, a pamphlet in the vein of Tom Paine's *The Age of Reason* remains unacceptable for many people around the globe.

---

[1] *Refer*: "Pamphleteering Literature" by George Orwell (1943).

The Fourth Estate

As these pages have attempted to outline, the evolution of English prose as the dynamic tongue of the pamphlet was driven by powerful socio-political and religious events allied with the technological innovation of the printing press as a machine that in turn drove cultural change.

The emergence of the periodical press or 'the press' as a platform by which to exert political influence is usually known as the 'fourth estate'. Thomas Carlyle in his *The French Revolution* (1837) attributes the term to Edmund Burke, who in this way alluded to the *three* Estates-General (*États généraux*) of feudal France: the clergy, the nobility, and the *bourgeoisie*. In a speech to Parliament, Mr Burke had evidently referred to those in the Reporters' Gallery as 'the fourth estate'.

In this early twenty-first century, there are those who would seek to control the evolution of the 'fourth estate' as the digital 'press' of the internet within the commanding heights or wayward rivers of the global economy. Along a mighty timeline, from Gutenberg to the present, a direct link is traceable from pamphlet to web page, with the twin spectres of propaganda and censorship haunting these media in the long struggle between free expression, with its tendency towards nonsense, and political power, with its inclination to lunacy and tyranny. As such, these aspects of society appear to be made for each other.

A Herring for
Robert Greene

A
QVIP FOR AN VP-
ſtart Courtier:

Or,

A quaint diſpute betvveen Veluet breeches
and Cloth-breeches.

*Wherein is plainely ſet downe the diſorders
in all Eſtates and Trades.*

LONDON
Imprinted by Iohn Wolfe, and are to bee ſold at his
ſhop at Poules chayne. 1 5 9 2.

Fig. 5 A Quip for an Upstart Courtier: A quaint dispute
between Velvet Breeches and Cloth breeches (1592) by Robert
Greene. The pamphlet is about country (cloth) versus city
(velvet) conventions. A certain Gabriel Harvey, a long-standing
nemesis of Greene, is the target. In "A Quip...", Greene fires his
broadside with obvious relish, which exploded in the midst of
the Harvey clan (who were from Essex).

ROBERT GREENE is remembered, if at all, as the hand behind a brief excerpt from an obscure pamphlet *A Groatsworth of Wit Bought with a Million of Repentance* (1592*)*. *A Groatsworth* was among Robert Greene's final outings as a pamphleteer, whereby he warns his readers against the ways of the 'low life' and the London underworld. For this reason, Greene had a reputation as something of a rogue, although this is primarily through association with that same 'low life' and the persistent evasion of his creditors.

In *A Groatsworth,* Greene warns (posthumously) of the dangers of dissipation and his repentance, and he should know, for a wasted life. In this general arena, Greene's knowledge had not been easily earned, but even so his wit costs a groat (lowest-denomination silver coin of the realm; one Groat=four English Pennies), which has then to be bought with a million in repentance. A kind of exchange rate has been established. The title is outstanding - one of the finest, tinged as it is with black humour and bitter regret - for a pamphlet. The subtitle does not leave much to spare, either: *Describing the folly of youth, the falsehoods of make-shift flatterers, the misery of the negligent, and the mischiefs of Courtesans.* What else does a provincial visiting London need to know? Robert Greene was well known among his gentlemen readers, who formed a ready-made audience for this kind of thing.

In that same year of 1592, Greene's two-part pamphlet appeared: *The Groundworke of Conny-catching* and *A Disputation between a Hee Conny-catcher and a She Conny-catcher.* In these texts, Greene again turns to his specialist subject: the 'low life'.

What, though, is a conny-catcher? From its obscure Welsh origins, 'conny' means rabbit, but Greene is not speaking here of those 'four leggers' (as the superstitious say). Greene is referring to the two-legged variety, the human victims of conmen and "the deceits of their Doxes" (women), such as cutpurses and cardsharpers, and so on, who would fleece the unwary. A human conny, like a rabbit, is easily skinned.

Robert Greene was always on the lookout for the ways of tricksters and villains, and his own creditors. He knew the ways of both. He employed at least one cutpurse by the sinister professional name of Cutting Ball, who was as quick with a dagger as his master's wit. Cutting Ball functioned as a shield between Greene and the creditors, and those servers of writs who likely lurked around the next corner. In a tavern on one occasion, so it was said, an unwary writ-server was made to eat his parchment (with wax seal to taste) from a plate. Where Cutting Ball provided protection, Greene had a mistress in the cutpurse's 'low life' sister, a whore, with whom he had a child. In this squalor, this Oxbridge scholar had sunk low, low, and lower yet. Greene knew of what he wrote. So be forewarned against these 'low life' creatures, he advised, or ruination will surely follow. His subject matter came to stick to him; he was stigmatised by it, and it by him.

For whatever reason, Greene's warnings appear to have been well intended. The pamphlets, then, as well as being a good read, were viewed as worldly advice for the naïve of London. They had better watch out. So said Robert Greene, pamphleteer and agony uncle of the Elizabethan age. In the wandering diatribe of *A Groatsworth of Wit*, Greene somehow finds space to issue a more esoteric kind of warning. This time, he addresses that literary elite known collectively as the University Wits. Greene, dissipated or not, stood among their ranks: Christopher

Marlowe (1564-1593), Thomas Nashe (1567-1601?), George Peele (1558?-1597?), *et al.* The warning, made almost in passing, refers to yet another kind of trickster: an "upstart crowe", who would threaten the very survival of "the best of you" as playwrights. Of this clique, the pioneering Marlowe likely had the most to lose, but then the Canterbury man would soon lose everything. In 1593, only a year after Greene's outburst, Marlowe had died in Deptford from a savage knife wound below the eye. The dispute over 'a reckoning' or bill for food and drink seemed a trivial cause for murder. A pretext, perhaps? Assassination, probably. Marlowe knew too much; he was too quick to speak his mind on unspeakable subjects (atheism, unnatural caresses, *etc*), and he knew too many things about Francis Walsingham (Elizabeth's spy-master), too. Kit Marlowe had been compromised - an obstacle, an embarrassment. Then, he was out of the way. Marlowe's passing seemed to open the way, too, for the emergence of another great playwright. This was, perhaps, the same "upstart crowe", a man of the provinces who stood with the stage, not a university, behind him. In the 1592 pamphlet, Greene had warned 'the Wits' of this new rival, and then died, even before the pamphlet had been published, but predeceasing Marlowe, who must, then, have set his eyes on *A Groatsworth.* In the famous excerpt, the parvenu "crowe" passes un-named, but he is *identified* as a player among players. A mere actor, with delusions of grandeur as a stage poet of blank verse. As with the conny-catchers, these actors are not to be trusted.

So imagine Greene in his garret with a pot of cheap Rhenish wine, no doubt brought by the long-suffering landlady Mrs Isam, as this unreliable tenant scratches-out these words:

> Yes, trust them not: for there is an upstart crowe,
> beautified with our feathers, that with a 'Tiger's
> heart wrapt in a player's hide'

Here, Greene supplies a distorted echo from the trilogy of plays *Henry VI,* where Queen Margaret, the "She-Wolf of France" is taunted further as "O Tiger's heart wrapt in a woman's hide".

The fragment is limned in acid, thus:

> - supposes he is as well able to bombast out a blank
> verse as the best of you;

This actor, it would seem, is also a presumptuous writer for the stage. So Greene, who spoke of himself as "of either university", is suggesting that the "upstart crow" is of neither university. Greene, though, is not yet done:

> And being an absolute *Johannes factotum*,

- An actor, not a scholar. A jobber. A player playing at play writing. A fellow of the stage who might turn his hand to anything - the words, too. There is much to consider here. Plays were being remade from the shattered shells or fragments of very old plays. In Renaissance Europe, the existence of ancient culture - or Antiquity - had been rediscovered. In Elizabethan England, Thomas Kydd and Christopher Marlowe had resurrected (revived is hardly the word) the Senecan tragedy. This is after Seneca (4 BC-65 AD): Roman philosopher and playwright, whose plays include *Oedipus*, *Medea*, and *Hercules.*

For the Elizabethan theatre, the dramatic tragedy was well served by the deployment of unrhymed iambic pentameters or blank verse, the legacy of Henry Howard, Earl of Surrey (c.1516?-*executed* 19 January 1547), courtier and poet, who had translated two books (the second and fourth) of the *Aenid* - and then sent to the block aged only thirty. . . In translation, the rhyme vanishes; the verse of Virgil's original is now *blank*, but highly effective. The innovation of the English stage had been to combine the tragedy with the potent instrument of blank verse for dramatic expression. A tradition had been established by Thomas Kydd with *A Spanish Tragedy* (c.1584-89) and Marlowe with *Doctor Faustus* (1588). Then, along came Shakespeare (seven years the younger than Greene), who represented the next step in the evolution of the English drama.

Now, in Greene's eyes, there was no stopping the bandwagon of actors. As the character assassination progresses, he writes in open code, less worthy of his genuine lyric gift, with a gross parody (if that is what this really is) of his subject's surname:

...is in his own conceit the only Shake-scene in the country.

And so *there* is the clue. The upstart is, surely, William Shakespeare, a provincial who had not attended either Oxford or Cambridge. The University Wits are about to be, or have already been, eclipsed. They have been outdone, beaten at their very own game. (As a writer, Shakespeare is the greatest of editors.) The progressive Elizabethan theatre had, for Greene, been purloined.

Robert Greene had raised the alarm, but it was too late. He was near death already. Poverty ingrained: lousy living conditions; dodgy wine; abominable food, of which pickled herring, said to be his last meal, turned his guts. In a most pitiful state, he succumbed to a general collapse of his faculties on 3 November 1592. In death as in life, the lice crawled through his scalp. As a tribute, Mrs Isam adhered with tradition: she placed bay or laurel leaves on the dead eyes of the copper-haired poet. Beside the corpse, a considerable body of work had been accumulated, which seemed to stand in mockery of Greene's wasted or impecunious life. And yet, he is remembered for this mere fragment - as though a pickled herring disgorged - from *A Groatsworth of Wit*, and printed (quickly, posthumously):

> Yes, trust them not: for there is an upstart crowe,
> beautified with our feathers, that with a 'Tiger's
> heart wrapt in a player's hide' supposes he is as
> well able to bombast out a blank verse as the best of
> you; ... is in his own conceit the only Shake-scene in
> the country.

> O that I might intreat your rare wits to be employed
> in a more profitable course: and let those apes
> imitate your past excellence, and never more
> acquaint them with your past inventions.

Robert Greene wrote of what he knew. But is this really Shakespeare, or some unknown actor as trickster, imitator - an Ape? (Greene, too, had been called an ape.) If this is the main target, then Robert Greene's cryptic early biography of Shakespeare is brief, uneasy, and savage in its intention.

The bitterness apparent in Greene's words might well stem from, not merely raw envy, but a more personal grudge. A good many of Greene's plays have been lost or are misattributed. Among these materials, there is a good chance that Greene had a hand in the development of earlier versions of the *Henry VI* cycle. As already cited, the

"upstart crowe" excerpt holds a line, embedded and
parodied, from Shakespeare's *Henry VI*. If this were so,
the younger man's dazzling success on the English stage
would have been all the more galling for Greene; for
Greene, of all people, would have been quick to recognise
that singular ability. As for the real identity of the upstart
actor, this must remain in the realm of conjecture.
Literary forensics so easily leads the investigator astray
into futile, though often lucrative, conspiracy theory. The
reality may well be more mundane. Greene must have
taken a good many 'newsworthy' items to his lonely grave
that would now seem revelatory. The excerpt, though,
remains a tease, the tirade being so brief; had Greene
dipped his quill that much deeper in the ink, scholars the
world over would have that much more to gorge on.
Instead, they have this tantalising morsel on which to
chew. The fragment both illuminates and obscures.

   In the eyes of conspiracy theorists everywhere,
Shakespeare looks like anyone but himself, which is
telling, but then Greene's reference seems to offer a real
man, with whom he was likely acquainted, as an actor -
playing the part of playwright - as the ape of the
University Wits. In *A Groatsworth*, Greene had also
written his own confessional and obituary: for a career as
poet, playwright, romancer - and, bitter to the end,
pamphleteer.

   Poor Robert Greene: he had been destitute, beyond his
means, and out of reach now of any debt collector or critic.
Greene's doublet and hose, as well as his sword, were sold
off for three shillings. But the cost of his burial came to 10s
4d. If Greene could not afford to live, then he could not
afford to die, either. His case serves as a warning to
anyone who would take up a pen with the intention of

earning a living. Shakespeare's achievement, then, appears the more remarkable. The Stratford man, though, was possessed of a peculiar insight beyond the reach even of Greene. In material terms, the great rival was to be found at the epicentre, as shareholder, of the popular commercial theatre: box office gold. As for Robert Greene, it was not as if he had not had his chance at the literary 'big time' of the day. That was how his life ended, but how had that life started?

ROBERT GREENE'S EARLY years were not so promising. As an adult, Greene seems streetwise; but, in the vein of most writers, he was (as his surname announces) a highly impressionable young man. He was born in Norwich, Norfolk, in 1555. A foundling, he was 'taken in' by a poor shoemaker and his wife, who subjected their young charge to a strict regime of plain living with a moral grounding. In this austerity, Greene somehow developed an aptitude, not for shoemaking, but for learning; and, in some way, he found himself on the high road of life bound for Cambridge University.

The foundling, then, had found his way - as a scholar, and a fledgling man of letters. In 1575, he entered St. John's College, where he graduated with a BA in 1579. By 1583, he was at Clare Hall with the award of Master of Arts. In about 1585, he found a wife - he called her "Dolly" - with whom he had a son. Greene deserted them both for wider horizons. In 1588, he was awarded a second MA, this time from Oxford University. In this way, Greene spoke of himself as "of either university". Robert Greene had come a long way since those early Norwich days.

Then, he disappears from the record. These are Greene's lost years, during which time he may have travelled in Europe. So, wherever he was and whatever he was doing in this interlude, he eventually ended up in London, among the players and printers. He must have known, and mixed with, the very best of them, and the worst of everyone else in the same *demi-monde* pond.

Robert Greene developed a special interest in, and propensity for, this *demi-monde* or half-world. So, he became a part of its fabric in an early version of Grub Street (now Ropemaker's Street in the City of London), where 'hacks', playwrights, poets, and printers colluded. The ways of the streets, too, provided him with source material for the pamphlets, if not the romances. From Greene's versatile quill flowed - or spewed - a stream of conceits, plays, and pamphlets. The bulk of these appeared (or disappeared) during the later period of his life, and immediately after his death. This was not for Greene or for posterity, but for printers looking to make a quick shilling over Greene's undemanding corpse. (Over the centuries, printers have not changed as much as their technology.)

In the reign of Elizabeth I, a considerable appetite existed for anything printed or performed, which had an aura of mystery, even magic. The printed word, if not read by the illiterate masses, could still be spoken by those who could read and heard by those who could not. This was a listening or aural society; an audience being those who *listen*. This was a revolution, printed or performed, that had ignited stages across Renaissance Europe. Robert Greene, wayward and debauched, was a part of this revolution. His output was impressive. If there is any anomaly about the man, then this was how the industrious Greene found the time for dissipation. The anomaly is, though, not so profound. Robert Greene needed money for wine, so he wrote for money, and so on, *etc*. The cyclical process, with its inevitable downward spiral, had a fatal outcome. Before that terminal decline, the wine-fuelled Greene wrote and wrote. So Greene made enough money to engage the 'low life' on his own terms. The wine, evidently, did not do him any good; the sordid pamphlets did not do his reputation any good, either.

Then look back a few years: in the poetry, or romantic verses, a genuine lyric gift is on display, and Greene's sensitive nature is seen to flourish. At intervals, the lyric verses cascaded to form the romances, among them such as: *The Mirror of Modesty* (1584), *Planetomachia* (1586), *Perimedes the Blacke-Smith* (1588); *Menaphon - Greens Arcadia* (1588), *Penelope's Web* and *Greene's Never Too Late* (both 1590), and *The Anatomie of Love's Flatteries* (1594). The players and playmakers all lived, sinking or swimming, in this same whirlpool: the romance *Pandasto, The Triumph of Time* (1588), though a prose romance, seems to provide a narrative scaffold for another playmaker's *A Winter's Tale* (c. 1616).

In Robert Greene's stagecraft, he confronted a challenge beyond mere confessional journalism, and his work for the Elizabethan stage is formidable. The plays include: *A Looking Glass for London and England* (with T. Lodge) *c.* 1590 (performed 1592) and the *Honorable Historie of Friar Bacon and Friar Bungay c.* 1580 (performed 1594). The title of this play, if not the play itself, somehow retains an easy familiarity. The tale of the two friars, no longer performed, is a highly entertaining burlesque on the always-engaging theme of alchemy. The first of these friars is Roger Bacon (*c.*1214-1294), a Franciscan monk, philosopher, and among the early empirical scientists. In the play, with some fine stagecraft by Greene, Friar Bacon is invested with extraordinary powers. The second friar is brother alchemist Thomas Bungay. The play remains highly readable. *Friar Bungay* overflows with warm good humour - unlike the humour-less *Dr Faustus* of Marlowe (from which it clearly derives).

The plays published within several years of Greene's passing, include: *The Scottish Historie of James Fourth* in 1598 and *The Comical Historie of Alphonsus King of Aragon* in 1599. In the 1590s, Greene's work appears to have found a popular audience, but for most of the decade he was not around to celebrate his own success. The wine would certainly have flowed in *those* years, and there may be more yet to the Greene canon than is realised. Scholars who look to this period have detected Greene's hand in other works. The play *A Knack to Know a Knave* (1592) has since been gifted to him, but this is inspired guesswork. The title, though, is *very* Greene-like. The play is anonymous, because the play - a satire on the State, or the state of society - was almost certainly (as with the long-lost *Isle of Dogs*) a threat to its author's well-being. A play about another Greene, *George-a-Greene, Pinner of Wakefield* (1599) has since been attributed to him, but this is, perhaps, starry-eyed conjecture. There is more evidence for, say, *King of Aragone*, since the title cover reveals the credit "RG" at a time when authorship was so often left to *Anon.* - or nobody, or only the printer or bookseller were named - so his byline must have had some pulling power, maybe. The question of attribution as a sales tool is, though, a curious matter. For instance, for the published quarto edition of the plays *The True Tragedie of Richard the third* (1594) and *King Leir and his three daughters* (1605) the author passes unacknowledged. The work of Robert Greene, then, is up there on the stage (though, for the most part, not in his lifetime) with "the best" of them. There is no question: Greene had a readership of 'Gents'; he was very popular.

This, from a bookseller's Preface:

The printer to the gentlemen readers.
Gentlemen, I know you are not unacquainted with the death of Robert Greene, whose pen in his lifetime pleased you as well on the stage as in the stationers' shops, and to speak truth, although his loose life was odious to God and offensive to men, yet forasmuch as at his last end he found it most grievous to himself . . .

. . .and so on, and then signed *C.B.* [Cuthbert Burby] by the bookseller, who was essentially cashing-in on a posthumous pamphlet - of which there were several - and, in this regard, even Greene's ghost was invoked to admonish his readers 'from beyond'. If ever there was a posthumous pamphleteer, then that was Robert Greene, *Esq.* There is truly no peace, or rest, then, for the wicked. A great many of Greene's 'gentlemen readers' were not interested in Greene as a person, dead or alive, but they were very curious about him and the world in which he moved. The dead-crafty Burby knew that much.

There is a sense in which greatness had eluded Greene: but he lacked preferment, and a Company, such that he had been diverted into the dangerous world of pamphleteering. As compared with the commercial 'high art' of play making, the pamphlets are those of a wayward, apolitical eccentric in need of vinous succour. These outpourings concern the folly of human beings, and an agitated desire for mending one's ways, the reform of one's character, or indeed what might now be called 'self-improvement', while he laments of the wasted existence (his own). Autobiography, this was not, but for subject matter Greene never had to stray very far away from Greene. More so than any other Elizabethan writer, Greene focused the dark lens of his insight on *himself*. This approach resulted in the pamphlets: *Greene's Morning Garment* (1590), *Greene's Farewell to Folly* (1591), and culminating with *A Groatsworths of Wit* (1592).

Hawk-eyed printers discovered the last of these among the detritus of Greene's room at Mrs Isam's establishment. The pamphlet appeared on 20 September 1592, barely a few weeks after its author had been buried at Bedlam churchyard. In this way, Greene seemed to speak from beyond the grave. This theme inspired the printers, and so Greene as a subject had distance yet. On 6 October 1592, *The Repentance of Robert Greene, Master of Arts* appeared: 'Printed for Cuthbert Burbie, and are to be sold at the middle shop in the Poultry under Saint Mildred's Church.' Robert Greene did not need to be paid; he was more profitable that way: dead. In death, cash still flowed out of Greene, with such as *Greene's Ghost Haunting Connie Catchers* (1601).

In his short life, Greene made friends, and lost friends - all of them. He made enemies, and kept them, even after death had taken him. The most corrosive of these was Gabriel Harvey, who despised Greene as an amoral fellow and a debaucher of the worst ilk. A man of low, and then lower, character. A whoremonger. Greene's powerful work ethic and obvious talent for a lyric meant nothing to Harvey. The entire Harvey clan hated Greene. Gabriel Harvey went out his way to call Greene "an Ape". This was a literary insult aimed at cutting Greene down to size: "the Ape of Euphues". This means nothing much today, but the *literati* of the time knew very well that this referred to John Lyly (1554-1606?), whose best-known work is

Euphues, The Anatomy of Wit (1579). Lyly's method had brought to the leaden English prose of the day a fresh, though artificial, style known as 'Euphuism' after the main character in *Anatomy*. The ornate style came in, bloomed, and then went out of fashion. Robert Greene and Thomas Nashe both abandoned 'the method' at an early date.

But for Harvey, Greene remained the "Ape of Euphues".

Who, though, was this Gabriel Harvey? The first point to acknowledge about Harvey is that he held the deepest of grudges against the highly educated outsiders Greene and Nashe, both of whom launched broadsides at the Harvey clan. In the pamphlet *A Quip for an Upstart Courtier* (1592), Greene fires his broadside with obvious relish, which explodes in the midst of the Harvey clan. The theme of country versus city living looks innocent enough at this distance; for the Harveys, though, who took themselves very seriously, the ridicule was unbearable. Robert Greene is out to have himself some sport, and sport he has. Along the way, any credibility the Harvey family might have had is demolished. The text presents a contrast between the high-born (velvet breeches, city) and plain living (cloth breeches, country). The protagonists are Gabriel Harvey's father and brothers; and, of course, Gabriel H. himself. The target is unnamed but clearly identified, identifiable: an Essex ropemaker and his sons. A fable of sorts, the piece relates of how, for some people, education is entirely wasted. Fools are to be educated; fools with money are to be better educated. Fools are to be sent to the University of Cambridge, no less, to become scholars and thinkers.

An outraged Gabriel Harvey had his revenge: with *Foure Letters and certain sonnets, especially touching*

upon Robert Greene and parties abused by him (1592).
This was his account of Greene's miserable downfall,
which must have required a close study of Greene's life,
and death · for the tract was published after its subject's
passing · about which Harvey surely had no qualms.

That last feast of cheap Rhenish wine and pickled
herrings, with its toxic shock to the gastric system, and
Greene was done for. (Thomas Nashe might have been an
eyewitness, although the two had fallen out by then.) In
Greene's final hours, he had written to his estranged wife,
with whom he had maintained remote contact over the
years. The heartbreak is almost tangible: "Dolly, I charge
thee, by the love of our youth, and by my soules rest that
you will see this man paide, for if he and his wife had not
succoured me I had died in the streets."

On the verge of death, Greene speaks here of "this man"
· the poor shoemaker, who had adopted this foundling.
From such a lowly background, it seems a miracle that
Greene had gotten anywhere near Cambridge and Oxford.
Then, step-by-step, he had gone to the dogs: to the reduced
circumstances of his early youth, and then from scholar to
squalor. In essence, Greene was a provincial who had
succumbed to the temptations of extra-curricular
university activities, before graduating to the London 'low
life'. (For the unwary, the same route is available to this
day.) This pre-disposition sealed his fate: a University Wit,
then an outcast. Highly emotional and impressionable, his
talent did not save him; it destroyed him · as did his
subject matter · and a herring. He was savvy, all right; the
emotional ballast is there, but only up to a point, and in
the wrong way.

Thomas Nashe, the younger contemporary, and fellow
pamphleteer, had this to say of his erstwhile friend in

Strange News or *Foure Letters Confuted*. The rebuke must have infuriated Gabriel Harvey to the point of apoplexy:

> "He inherited more virtues than vices. A jolly long red peak - like the spire of a steeple - he cherished continually without cutting. . .He had his faults, and thou [Gabriel Harvey, who else?] and thy follies. Debt and deadly sin, who is not subject to? With any notorious crime I never knew him tainted. . a jolly good fellow he was. . .
> … and would have drunk with thee [Harvey]. . . and in one year pissed against the walls as thou and thy two brothers spent in three.
> …In a night and a day, would he have yarked up a pamphlet as well as in seven year; and glad was the printer that might be so best to pay him for the very dregs of his wit. . .
> . . . He made no account of winning credit by his works as thou dost that dost no good works. . . His only care was to have a spell in his purse to conjure up a good cup of wine with at all times."

The hilarious encounter with the Harveys sparkles darkly as a warning to those inclined to take themselves a little too seriously.

As the leader among those *avante-garde* 'journalists' (when no such term existed), Robert Greene casts a longer shadow, albeit a shadow, than most of his associates, and every one of his critics, could ever have known. The reference to the "upstart crowe", rightly or wrongly in its inference by some scholars, will last for as long as books on the elusive Master Shakespeare are written. As for the two friars Bacon and Bungay, the play might yet see its day in the sun, when the world is inclined to recognise its own wayward and original spirit in its son, Robert Greene.

An Almond for
Thomas Nashe

THOMAS NASHE is the archetype for the role of English novelist and feature journalist. In an age when no such terms were known, Nashe is remembered for *The Unfortunate Traveller* (1594), an innovation for English prose, since the novel form did not really exist beyond continental Europe. Exceptions are found with Edmund Malory's *Mort d'Arthur* (1485), which is not really a novel but a cycle of romances, published by William Caxton, and Thomas More's *Utopia* (1516) albeit in Latin. *The Unfortunate Traveller* is distinct as a picaresque thriller, with the subtitle *The Life of Jack Wilton*. The narrative chronicles the adventures of its rakish hero, whom Nashe propels across France, Italy, and Germany, where he encounters the famous and infamous from history, and then returns to London. The *realism* of the text, that is, the depiction of actual lived experience, is far ahead of its time, since this vivid approach did not take root in English letters until the much later arrival of Daniel Defoe.

The son of a clergyman, Thomas Nashe was born in 1567 at Lowestoft, Suffolk. The family later moved to West Harling in Norfolk. In 1582, Nashe went up to St John's College, Cambridge (he revelled in this seat of learning) and by 1586 had taken his BA. In about 1588, he travelled to London, and he may also have journeyed through Europe in this interval.

As with Christopher Marlowe, Robert Greene, and George Peele, *et. al.*, Thomas Nashe counted among the ranks of the University Wits. In many ways, he was a quill for hire. For this reason, controversy sought out Nashe as much as he sought out controversy. Nashe produced a play, extended prose works, and pamphlets; he was, perhaps, far too good-natured to be a great writer, but he was way ahead of his time as a feature journalist and novelist. The single play Nashe wrote is *Summer's Last Will and Testament* (1600). Even by his own standards, he was not much of a playwright, but he was a very good fixer and patcher-up, and so did not shrink or shirk from the daunting task of completing Kit Marlowe's unfinished play *Dido, Queen of Carthage*. How much of the text might be attributed to Nashe is speculative.

Another play of this era had even more unseen hands in its construction, which makes for an intriguing case study in the power of censorship as exercised through the Privy Council and the apparatus of the Elizabethan state. Of the play *Isle of Dogs* (1597), only the title survives as a vestige of its erasure from the record. The text of the play vanished, and has not to date been rediscovered. That the play was staged at all is perhaps surprising, since any performance of dramatic scripts required approval from the Master of the Revels. The Isle of Dogs? This was once an isle that is today the largest meander in the River Thames (to the north, West India Docks). In the hands of the playmakers, though, *Isle of Dogs,* might also be taken for the island of Britain, a state that could be said to be 'going to the dogs'. This was a dangerous game to play for those of the theatre world so easily identifiable. "Seditious and slanderous utterances," declaimed the authorities. The play was closed by order of the Privy Council, and its principal author and editor Ben Jonson (1573-1637) identified. Off-stage, as it were, Johnson was arrested, cross-examined, and imprisoned at the Marshalsea.

Among the play's most likely co-authors, Thomas Nashe seems to have found a temporary refuge outside of London with a bolthole in Great Yarmouth, there to conduct a study of the history of that town and its herring industry; this, while the real-life drama of Ben Johnson incarcerated was being enacted elsewhere. There had been times, though, when the likes of Nashe, learned, with a ready wit, and part-deadly with a quill, had displayed a talent as propagandists: either for literary disputation, the powder keg of religious controversy, or indeed secular feud.

Thomas Nashe entered the world of pamphleteering as the author of a preface: for Robert Greene's *Menaphon* (1589). As a literary argument, the purpose now seems trivial, unless this is to establish the reputations of the authors. This is accomplished at the expense of more seasoned writers, such as Kydd, whose style by this time was perceived as affected, fanciful, or mannered - as seen by these young upstarts. In its essence, the *Menaphon* is a challenge (by Greene and supported by Nashe) to the established literary cliques of London. The time had come to move on, and the way ahead had already been opened, not by Greene and Nashe, but by a covert writer.

The roots for an early form of journalism are located within a more complex affair known as the Martin Prelate Controversy, with which both Nashe and probably Greene were involved as hired 'hacks' in the battle of ideas - and nerves - between two main factions: the fanatical Puritans and the mighty bishops of the established Church of England.

The Martin Prelate or *Mar*prelate (*i.e.,* suggestive of bishop bashing) Controversy originated in 1583 with the appointment of the formidable John Whitgift (who was no friend of the Puritans) to the high seat of Archbishop of Canterbury. The reaction from the puritans: *A Learned Discourse* (the full title is excruciating), which made the case for reform (away with all taint of Popery, *etc.*, *etc.*) in 1584.

The royal church was under attack, and an ill-natured battle of propaganda ensued.

By 1586, John Whitgift had joined forces with the Bishop of London, Richard Bancroft, to invoke a Star Chamber decree to censure unlicensed printing. The reaction? Pamphlets continued to spew from underground presses, with the key titles appearing under the pseudonym of "Martin Prelate" as extremist reformer and mouthpiece of the Puritans.

The prose style is refreshingly witty and cutting, albeit many Puritans took offence at such ribald word-play. The form of expression is quaintly ironical in its subversion of the bishops and the royal church. Nothing quite like this had been seen before, and the pamphlets were gobbled-up by the popular audience. These tracts augur the birth of an early form of journalistic satire to prefigure, by more than a century, the style of Swift's *Tale of a Tub*. The high church clergy felt compelled to reply in the same vein, but who, though, might use a quill as a weapon with the same skill as the mysterious "Martin?" Who else? Thomas Nashe and Robert Greene, these two literary blades in need of a regular income, with their unlikely Episcopal sponsors. An anti-puritan by nature, Nashe seems to have been extraordinarily well placed to take on this potentially dangerous assignment. After the appearance of the highly effective (to the delight of the Puritans) *Learned Discourse* and the invocation of the old Star Chamber decree (to the great joy of the bishops), the chronology is complex. The asperities of the disputation are obscured and eroded by the passage of time, but some peaks in the cycle remain visible.

The next salvo of pamphlets incurred the wrath of the Star Chamber: *The Aequity of a Humble Supplication*

(1587) by John Penry and the anonymous *Diotrephes* (1588) masked the identity of John Udall. As the campaign intensified, with many blasts against the bishops, Nashe was drawn into the role of propagandist against 'Martin'. The extent of Nashe's contribution remains unclear. The replies to "Martin's" broadsides, which are inferior, include such as *A Countercuffe Given by Martin Junior* (1589). The counter-attacks also adopted the figure of "Pasquill" in such tracts as *The Return of Pasquill* (1589) and *The First Prate of Pasquill's Apologie* (1590). The quaintly titled *An Almond for a Parrot* (1590) is probably by Nashe.

The controversy eventually imploded or digested itself on 'Martin's' side with *The Protestatyon of Martin Prelate* (1589). The secret presses were located and impounded; the printers were imprisoned. John Penry was eventually captured and executed. "Martin Prelate" disappeared, although suspicion became attached to the names of Job Throckmorton and Sir Richard Knight. The Marprelate Controversy might have been over, but the bishops had developed a sophisticated taste for censorship that would eventually lead to the Bishops' Ban of 1599 with the burning of books.

As for Thomas Nashe, the campaign had provided him with most exceptional and valuable experience by parroting, and then improving on, the original style of the insidious 'Martin Prelate'. In this way, he formulated a method - the "extemporal vein", he liked to say - by which to take on the challenge, self-imposed, of his immediate post-Marprelate pamphlets.

Away from the controversial, the daily grind of Nashe's penury - in the way of Robert Greene - was also a readily available subject for explication. On the matter of poverty or cash paucity, anyway, the good-natured Nashe had plenty of experience. "The seven liberal sciences," a rueful Nashe once remarked, "and a good leg will scarce get a scholar bread and cheese." So much for Nashe's reputation as a fast-living scribe; he was so cash-strapped that he even turned to a sub-genre to eke out the most basic living, and basic could be most base indeed. On occasion, he would try his hand at writing priapic 'ditties' as a form of stimulating reading for 'gentlemen'. The innocent-seeming *Choosing of Valentines* is nothing of the sort. A romance? Not exactly. A rich imagination made up for a lack of direct experience of the usually grim enough reality. So Nashe had stooped low to write for the wayward appetites of paying gentlemen. There is no romantic intent to these pieces; he was not a romancer in the early vein of the later debauched Greene. On the balance of his character, though, he was not good at being 'a hater' or even a curmudgeon like Gabriel Harvey. Thomas Nashe: destitute quill for hire. An associate of the time recounted: ". . .never in his life a shoemaker or a tailor." As he was able, Nashe turned such hardship into a few coins. The titles speak for themselves: *Pierce Pennilesse his Supplication to the Devil* (1592) and *The Apology of Pierce Pennilesse* (1593).

For his next project, Nashe turned to the occult with *Terrors of the Night or A Discourse on Apparitions* (1594). The title is almost a guarantee, then as now, of a popular audience. Nashe peered into the darkness, which he found populated by legion demons. A powerful imagination is seen at work, there is no doubt, and Nashe explores his spectral theme through the eyes of an old man recently retired to the deathbed of his chamber. As the story begins, the old man closes his eyelids, and is besieged by a series of apparitions: silver nets and hooks (the devil 'a-fishing' in the night); a company of sailors on shore leave with strong drink on offer; a group of demons make an appearance, followed by the devil himself, with temptation by way of a troupe of naked virgins: "Their hair they ware loose unrolled about their shoulders . . ." In a scene to shock the unworldly, female devils appear dressed as nuns. After two days of this torment, the feverish old man expires. Nashe's dream sequence along the final frontier is done. This was a highly unusual experiment in prose for its day, with a psychological dimension of the dream state. Nashe seems to have composed the tract during a pleasant interlude on the Isle of Wight while based at Carisbrooke Castle, the family seat of Sir George Cary. So, there is evidence here for Nashe having had a patron for a time. *Terrors of the Night* is dedicated to "Elizabeth", Sir George's daughter.

Nashe continued to explore his prose method with the revelatory *Christ's Tears Over Jerusalem* (1593). The tract, with its enigmatic title, is essentially a plague pamphlet - a warning. As Jerusalem had fallen as a punishment by God, then so, too, might London with its population of sinners. By the early 1590s, Nashe had become embroiled in a protracted pamphleteering feud with the die-hard bachelor-scholar Gabriel Harvey. The quarrel concerned Nashe's erstwhile friend, Robert Greene, who had been unable to resist ridiculing the Harveys (who had taken exception to *Menaphon*) with *A Quip from an Upstart Courtier* (1592). The short squib had pointed to that family's humble background as the sons of an Essex ropemaker. Education, Greene had asserted, is wasted on some people (the Harveys). Gabriel Harvey, incandescent with rage, sought vengeance, though Greene had recently died aged thirty-six. That plain fact did not deter Harvey, who launched a vicious assault on the low character of the dead man with *Foure Letters* (1592). The style, so it was said, was that of a "crab tree cudgel". In defence of his old friend, Nashe responded with *Strange News* or *Foure Letters Confuted* (1592). The feud persisted well into the decade. A direct broadside on the Harveys took the form of *Have with You to Saffron Walden* (1596). A counter-attack appeared with *The Trimming of Thomas Nashe, Gentlemen* (1597). This has often been misattributed to Harvey, but the real author (unless a stalking-horse for Harvey?) is Richard Lichfield, a barber-surgeon of Cambridge, who was also in that capacity some sort of wit and entertainer. Of special interest, the only surviving image of Nashe appears as a frontispiece to this tract: a woodcut with Nashe in notional shackles (as Harvey would have him) and his old nemesis in possession of the key.

The character of Gabriel Harvey (c. 1545? - 1630) should now be explained away. Born at Saffron Walden in Essex, Harvey was the son of a master ropemaker. A Cambridge man (Christ's College, BA 1570), the scholarly Harvey quarrelled with nearly everyone, and ruined his own latent literary gifts as a poet and prose master with a curmudgeonly disposition; otherwise, he may well have left his mark in the sparkling firmament of the Elizabethan literary world. What Harvey wanted, he did not get, which was an adherence to a Latin tradition as a bulwark against what he saw as the encroachment of the 'barbaric' English tongue. The view was widely held: English was the vulgar or spoken word of the common herd. Harvey wanted, of all things, English hexameters. Harvey fought for this vision, with his innate ability to make his associates and colleagues highly uncomfortable. The nearest he had to 'a friend' (to stretch the definition) was the long-suffering Edmund Spencer, whose epic poem *The Faerie Queen* (for which Spencer invented the 'stanza') Harvey almost scuttled with his warped advice. The 'advice' was especially insidious, since Harvey, though ill natured, had a reputation as an outstanding scholar. The stoical Spencer, with a measure of diplomacy, survived the encounter, and so the *Faerie Queene* lives eternal. Gabriel Harvey is remembered, not primarily as an Elizabethan scholar of note, but as an embittered man who seems to dance yet on the graves of Nashe and Greene, and he is made for the part.

In 1599, the pamphleteering feud was terminated by the decree known as 'The Bishops' Ban, and in which the paper duellists are cited, thus:

> "All of Nasshes bookes and Doctor Harveyes bookes
> be taken whersoever they maybe found and that
> none of their books bee ever printed hereafter. . ."

The bishops reveal a certain irritability here, since the feud, this time around, is of a strictly secular nature. The 'hereafter' is a long time for a writer of gusto and imagination such as Nashe, and his precarious career took a final turn into obscurity. In this interval, Nashe had reached not so much a crossroads as a terminus, but he had one more outing as a pamphleteer in the pipeline immediately prior to the Bishops' Ban.

In 1597, the scandal of *Isle of Dogs* had outraged the Privy Council. The authorities had even searched Nashe's lodgings for manuscript evidence of a script. As for the lodger, he had already made a hasty exit from London for Great Yarmouth, ostensibly to write about herrings. In

Elizabethan England, the herring of the Dogger Bank was
a crucial source of protein, and very big business in
London. The pamphlet is *Nashe's Lenten Stuff* (1599),
which is widely referenced as an evocation of Yarmouth
and its herring industry. The tract, though, is something
of a red herring itself, with idiosyncratic diversions and
allusions, such as:

> " . . .how the herring first came to be a fish, and
> then how he came to be King of the Fishes. . . how
> from white to red he changed, would require as
> massy a tome as Holinshed; but in half-a-penny
> worth of paper I will epitomize them."

Thomas Nashe, along with Robert Greene, pioneered
an early form of feature journalism, with which he tackled
an eclectic and at times strangely engaging choice of
subject matter from spooks in the night to the fishes of the
sea. In his final years, Thomas Nashe found anonymity.
He is thought never to have married. The last track of his
life is obscure, and he died in about 1601.

The poet John Dryden, looking back on that
extraordinary decade of the 1590s, had warm words for
Thomas Nashe: "A breach of the laurel well deserved to
bear," which serves as a worthy epitaph in the journey of
this unfortunate traveller.

Thomas Dekker
at the Mermaid Tavern

FOR THOSE PLAYMAKERS who might have attempted to follow Christopher Marlowe's dangerously ambitious trajectory, daily life took on a more familiar pattern: from the 'ordinary' or eating-house, thence to the stage, and onward for the tavern, and so the cycle continued. Beyond, fame and fortune (that needed plenty of luck, unnatural talent, daring, and patronage) or there was the more likely path *via* the debtors' prison to obscurity.

In the interim, there was the tavern. In one such watering hole, the famous Mermaid Tavern, the play-makers crowded together to drink and talk of theatrical intrigue:

> "What things we have seen
> Done at the Mermaid Tavern! heard words that have been
> So nimble, and so full of subtle flame,
> As if that everyone from whence they came
> Had meant to put his whole wit in jest,
> And had resolved to live a fool the rest
> Of his dull life."

> ~ *Master Francis Beaumont to Ben Jonson.*

In the way of all good inns, The Mermaid Tavern[1] had a strategic *locale*: in London's Cheapside, just East of St Paul's, on the corner of Bread Street and Friday Street, which gave its name to the legendary Friday Club, purportedly founded by Sir Walter Raleigh in 1603. In those years, the landlord was William Johnson, and his distinguished clientele is said to have included Ben Jonson and William Shakespeare (engaged in the cross-fire of literary banter), Marlowe, Nashe, Greene · and, most

---

[1] The Mermaid was destroyed in the Great Fire of London (1666).

probably, Thomas Dekker. As with Robert Greene, Dekker's output was considerable, and his books, plays, and pamphlets have survived the passage of time since the 1590s and early 1600s. Dekker certainly made his mark, and some of his plays were performed by Court Order before Elizabeth I. As author and collaborator in over forty plays, Dekker played a leading role in what became known as the War of the Theatres. Effectively triggered by the Bishops' Ban of 1599 on printed matter of a satirical vein, the stage remained as the primary outlet for such expressions, and so impresarios fought for dominance of this commercial audience.

James Burbage had founded The Theatre in 1576, among the very first (along with the Red Lion) dedicated performance venues in England since the Roman occupation. In Dekker's day, the most famous theatres (and all required a licence) were: The Rose; The Fortune; The Globe, where the Lord Chamberlaine's Men performed the plays of Shakespeare, *et. al.;* the famous Swan Theatre (where the seditious *Isle of Dogs* was briefly performed); and the second Blackfriars Theatre.

The dramatic war, whether real or contrived promotional stunt, was one of intense rivalry. These venues, among others, formed the battleground for the rivalry, with Dekker and Ben Jonson on opposing sides. Dekker wrote for The Admiral's Men, who usually performed at The Fortune, co-managed by Philip Henslowe (1550-1616) with the great actor Edward Alleyne, who determined that he had spent the princely sum of £1,300 on acquiring the lease in 1599.

After two decades, The Fortune was destroyed by fire on 9 December 1621.

The War of the Theatres and its series of competing

plays, or what Dekker termed the *Poetomachia,* continued until about 1602.

DEKKER OR DECKER: the name is likely of Dutch origin; and, a London-man possibly of Southwark, he seems to know about aspects of the Netherlands. The details of his birth (1572?), life and death (1632?) are obscure. For biographical insights, the man emerges as no more than a silhouette; otherwise, the Prefaces of the plays provide some clues as to his character.

Dekker's embryonic reputation as something of a genius of the Elizabethan stage is brought crashing down to earth by Henslowe's diary (a source of rich pickings for researchers of this era), with the entry for January 1597, where a "Mr Dickers" is cited in respect of "twenty shillings" for the acquisition of a play script. After two more diary entries, "Mr Dickers" or Dekker disappears, and so a promising career is made and unmade. There are debts to be paid; but a playwright in debtors' jail is not much good to anyone (and certainly not the creditors). Just over a year later, Henslowe writes: "Lent unto the company, the 4 of February 1598, to discharge Mr. Dicker owt of the cownter of the powltry, the some of fortie shillings. I saye dd [delivered] to Thomas Dowton [some kind of agent or go-between]. . . xxxx." This grim enough citation related to Dekker being lodged at the Powltry for debt (today, Poultry Street in the City, between Mansion House and Bank).

As for Henslowe, he had his methods:

"Should these fellowes come out of my debt, I should have no rule over them."

In one single internment, Dekker appears to have spent the years 1613-1616, or even longer, in confinement.

There is a real sense, though, that Dekker took his incarceration and many other setbacks with a measure of good humour. A playmaker in prison? The stage is well set, then. What choice had he, really? The very well-heeled Henslowe helped, and helped again, but a precarious existence is writing for the stage. The familiar cycle ordinary-stage-tavern often had a postscript: prison for debt or dissent, grinding poverty, and an early death. In his way, though, Dekker (like Nashe) was almost too good-natured; this marred his work, where a tincture of the Marlowesque (though Marlowe's influence is certainly there) darkness might have offset, for relief, those sunny urban pastures. An extraordinary character in one of his own plays, Dekker vanishes off-stage under the same yellow sky.

What, then, of Dekker's plays? The Dekker canon is substantial, impressive. The collected dramatic works occupy four volumes. The two parts of *The Honest Whore* are separated in time (1604 & 1630) by a quarter of a century. The plays also feature *The Shoemaker's Holiday* (1599), the good-humoured *Will's Last Summer* (1599), *Old Fortunatus* (published 1600), and of special interest *Match Me in London* (eventually published in 1631). Dekker also collaborated in play-making ventures, most notably *The Spanish Moor's Tragedy* (probably with Houghton and Day), and possibly *Lust's Dominion.* In its totality, Dekker's output is panoramic. As with the rare case of Robert Greene, Dekker remains outstanding in that, unlike many dramatists of this era, his legacy also includes a considerable body of prose.

An overview of the non-dramatic works is provided by Dr Goshart's edition (1885-86) of Dekker's prose, which takes up five volumes. Outstanding in the *oeuvre, The*

Gull's Horn Book flaps for attention in 1590. In this extended prose work, Dekker acts as guide and advisor to the young blades or *Gallants* and the tavern-going theatricals of London. One chapter advises on "How a Gallant Should Behave himself in an Ordinary"; this is followed by, along that same daily cycle, "How a Gallant should behave himself in the Playhouse". Yet another chapter relates advice for the Poet who might repair to the Ordinary:

> "Observe no man; doff not a cap to that gentle-man today at dinner, to whom, not two nights since, you were beholden for a dinner…"

In other words, you had to make the proper entrance to form the right impression. In this way, the ordinary and the tavern, then, were stages, too, in the way of the theatre. In quite some detail, Dekker goes on to define a code of conduct for those who frequented these establishments. There must have been an audience for this kind of narrative, although Dekker appears to be addressing his own inner circle - or, indeed, a wider audience of would-be gallants. As a social document of that *milieu*, *The Gull* is that rare thing indeed: an eyewitness account of this slice of Elizabethan life in the form of what would now be termed social commentary.

Dekker's pamphleteering earns him a place among the proto-journalists. A great deal of his output survives, including: *Seven Deadly Sinnes of London* (1606), a theme once explored by Nashe; and *Newes from Hell* (1606), among many others.

As with Thomas Nashe, Dekker's prose conveys a realism to pre-figure the journalism, a century later, of Daniel Defoe. For instance, *A Wonderful Year* (1603) turns out to be a plague pamphlet for a city so stricken at the time. The title, though, alludes to the year of succession, and there is some evidence that Dekker may well have helped with plans for the street entertainments as the procession of James I entered the city of London. In general, though, the narrative thread running through the pamphlets is that of a good-natured observer, never malicious, surveying London street-life with an insider's knowledge, so often slap-dash, let loose on his subject matter, which offers insights of the playmakers and tradesmen and tradeswomen of his day (the shoemaker, the seamstress, the master tailor), and of a life that has long since been obscured. As playmaker and chronicler of the 'ordinary', he may not have possessed the "mighty line" of Kitt Marlowe, but Thomas Dekker retains his own sunny uplands and stands there among the world's earliest reporters.

THE FIRST
BLAST OF THE
TRUMPET AGAINST
THE MONSTRVOVS
regiment of
women.
*

Veritas temporis
filia.

M· D· LVIII·

Fig. 6, 7 & 8: John Knox (1510-1572) went too far with his ill-advised *The First Blast of the Trumpet Against the Monstrous Regiment of Women* (1558, Geneva). The pamphlet is an attack on the female monarchs of Europe, primarily with Mary Tudor in his sights. An exercise in high-level misogyny, *First Blast* backfired in Knox's face when Mary's half-sister ascended the English throne that same year. Elizabeth I was not entirely amused.

Fig. 9 Robert Greene (1558-1592): in this woodcut, Greene is depicted hard at work, albeit he is already dead with the death- shroud as improvised headgear. As England's first working 'journalist', he had a popular audience, but with the reputation of a 'low life'.

The debauched Greene's impressive output included romances, plays, and pamphlets. Thomas Nashe reported that Greene had expired after a feast of cheap Rhenish wine and pickled herring. . . Greene is chiefly remembered, if at all, for his alchemical play *Friar Bacon, Friar Bungay* (*c.* 1580) and a fragment from a pamphlet . . .

Fig. 10 *A Groatsworth of Wit bought with a Million of Repentance* (1592) is among Greene's last pamphlets. The tract remains famous among scholars for an excerpt about an actor-playwright referred to as "an upstart crowe. . .The only Shake-scene in the country." After the death of Greene, this and other pamphlets were plundered from his lodgings and rushed into print.

An Almond for a Parrat,
Or
Cutbert Curry-knaues
Almes.

Fit for the knaue Martin, and the
rest of those impudent Beggers, that
can not be content to stay their stomakes
with a Benefice, but they will needes
breake their fastes with
our Bishops.

Rimarum sum plenus.

Therefore beware (gentle Reader) you
catch not the hicket with laughing.

Imprinted at a Place, not farre from
a Place, by the Assignes of Signior Some-body, and
are to be fold at his shoppe in Trouble-knaue
street, at the signe of the
Standish.

THE
Terrors of the night
Or,
A Discourse of Apparitions.

Post Tenebras Dies.

THO: NASHE.

LONDON,
Printed by *Iohn Danter* for *William Iones*, and are to be fold
at the signe of the Gunne nere Holburne Conduit.
1594.

Fig. 11 *An Almond for a Parrot* (1590) appeared in the closing stages of Martin Prelate Controversy (attributed to Thomas Nashe). In the pamphleteering warfare between fanatical puritans and the established Church of England, the bishops were ridiculed by "Martin", who wrote with an easy, witty style - that is, satirical.

The bishops turned to Nashe and Greene, *et. al.*, to produce rebukes, but none were as spontaneous or as successful as the pamphlets of the mysterious "Martin". The affair ended when agents of the Stationers' Company located the secret presses of the puritans. The printer, a Mr John Penry, was executed in 1593. Nashe inherited the legacy of 'Martin', with the birth of an early form of feature journalism.

Thomas Nashe, with the deadly experience of the pamphlete-ering warfare behind him, developed his prose method with such tracts as:

Fig. 12 *Terrors of the Night* (1594), which shows a powerful imagination at work with its glimpse into the spectral world.

THE
TRIMMING
of Thomas Nashe Gentleman,
by the high-titled patron *Don*
Richardo de Medico campo, Barber
Chirurgion to Trinitie Col-
ledge in Cambridge.

Faber quas fecit compedes ipse gestat.

LONDON,
Printed for Philip Scarlet.
1597.

Fig. 13 Thomas Nashe (1567-1601) and his nemesis **Gabriel Harvey** (1545–1630), who withholds the key to Nashe's shackles (as his critics would have him). A distinguished academic, but a curmudgeon, Harvey's *Foure Letters* had attacked Nashe's friend Robert Greene (deceased).

Source: The woodcut (*top, right*) is reproduced in the hatchet-job . . .

Fig. 14 *The Trimming of Thomas Nashe, Gentlemen* (1597), which has sometimes been misattributed to Harvey; and, although part of the ongoing feud, the tract is probably by Richard Lichfield, a barber-surgeon of Cambridge.

Fig. 15 *Nashe's Lenten Stuffe* (1599) *over*: 'Lenten stuff'? Food for Lent. An evocation of Great Yarmouth and its herring industry, the tract represents an early form of feature journalism, with plenty of red herrings, too.
After the Bishops' Ban of 1599, this was Thomas Nashe's final outing as a pamphleteer.

NASHES

Lenten Stuffe,

Containing,

**The Defcription and firft Procrea-
tion and Increafe of the towne of**
Great Yarmouth in
Norffolke:

With a new Play neuer played before, of the
praife of the RED
HERRING.

*Fitte of all Clearkes of Noblemens Kitchins to be
read: and not vnneceffary by all Seruing men
that hauefhort boord-wages, to be remembred.*

Famam peto per vndas.

LONDON
Printed for N. L. and C. B. and are to be
fold at the weft end of Paules.
1599.

L

John Milton
and the *Areopagitica*

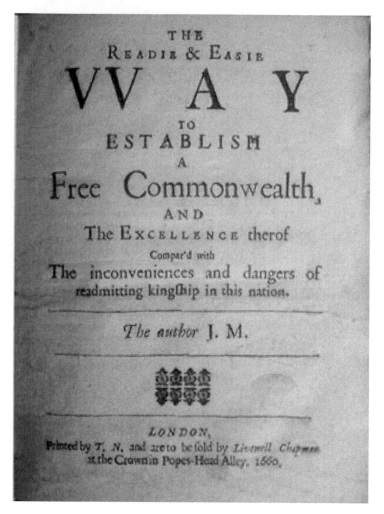

Fig. 16 Readie and Easie Way to Establish a Free Commonwealth (1660) by "JM". As Latin Secretary (chief apologist-propagandist) for the Cromwell regime, John Milton - "JM" - had a narrow escape from the gallows with the Restoration (1661) of Charles II, and so lived to compose or rather dictate *Paradise Lost* (1667) in blind old age. There were those among the superstitious who believed God had blinded Milton for his part in the Interregnum.

JOHN MILTON: the name is plain enough, and yet somehow speaks of vaulting ambition and the greatest of all themes: paradise and damnation, perhaps even redemption, and of the transient nature of human being-ness across the span of birth and death, and even the afterlife. The Interregnum or Commonwealth era captured the body and soul of John Milton, who witnessed the Restoration of the monarchy in England; and, by some grace, after a narrow escape from the gallows, lived to experience the final release in opaque blind old age of his gifts as a poet of visionary power with the epic poems *Paradise Lost* and *Paradise Regained*, and the dramatic poem *Samson Agonistes*, wherein the strongman, his eyes put out, wanders "eyeless in Gaza" - by which time Milton was as blind as his protagonist.

The achievement is transcendental. John Milton gifted the phrase "fame is the spur" to the English language; this is to be found in the poem *Lycidas* (1638), and so it went with its author.

If his subject was the possibilities inherent in the human spirit as a force in nature, then John Milton had to cast an inward eye on his own imagination. For a boy and then man of his disposition - high-minded, remote, aloof - this cannot have been easy, but the passion and imagination, deep within Milton, is an untold story in every human as a sacrifice to society. Then again: the journey must start somewhere.

John Milton was born at Bread Street in the Cheapside area of London on 9th December 1608 to John Milton, a scrivener or notary, and Sarah Jeffrey. An old Oxfordshire family, the Miltons had disinherited the scrivener for straying from the traditional Catholic fold to follow the ways of the Reformed Church in England. The younger

John Milton grew up in a twilight world of an England in flux as the struggle between the established Church and Puritan extremists intensified on the road to the English Revolution. The boy Milton grew up in a cosseted atmosphere afforded by his father's lucrative profession, without which there might not have been any poet by the name of Milton or any such poem as *Paradise Lost*. The years passed by with the early training of a poet, reading deep into the night by candlelight, and writing juvenile (though not by his standards) verses in both Latin and English. This was not a normalized childhood. If this were precocity, there was also unnatural hard graft, by which he forged an independence of mind not easily won at any age in any era. The Milton identity soon emerged: he took himself, and his efforts, extremely seriously; he was primarily interested in himself (but perhaps not in the way this might mean today).

After the self-study and private tutoring, the nine-year-old Milton entered St. Paul's School in 1620. By 1624, the thirteen-year-old had reached Cambridge University. After the relative comfort and privacy of the scrivener's home (Milton senior had since retired to Buckinghamshire), the strict regime and Spartan existence of the scholastic life was not entirely to Milton's taste, and in return he was generally disliked or misunderstood. Milton must have seemed a strange cove indeed to his fellow students; his effeminate appearance earned him the sobriquet "The Lady of Christ's" [College]. "The Lady" did not get on too well with his tutor, either. As the would-be author of his own curriculum, Milton had ideas of his own; at one stage, there was a long period of absenteeism. In any event, he took his MA in 1632, and then re-joined the family in Buckinghamshire. By this time he was writing serious poetry. In this interval, Milton composed the elegy *Lycidus,* which came to be included in the Christ's College memorial volume. As for the choice of a career, he was in no great hurry. Milton first decided to undertake a tour of Europe; this was *de rigueur* for young gentlemen of a certain background. So off he set in 1638. Destination: *via* Paris, where else but Florence, crucible of the Renaissance, where Milton's knowledge of classical languages might be enriched, and himself more appreciated. As the traveller leaves the shores of England, then so time is suspended; and in this continuum, while Milton was adrift on the Continent, the political situation in England deteriorated as the country set itself firmly on the course for civil war.

In Florence, Milton took time to furnish his mind as an aristocrat might furnish a mansion house: with great paintings, the literature of ages, conversations un-paralleled, and meetings with famous men. In this way, he met with Galileo, under house arrest for heresy, and blind with age (the same fate that awaited this young Englishman). Then, Milton's conscience prickled: who was he to absent himself in Florence while his countrymen faced almost certain calamity at home? In England, the outcome was far from clear; anything might happen, and so Milton found passage back to a home port in July 1639, not to pursue the vocation of poet, but to make an unlikely name as a famous, or if not an infamous, pamphleteer. That same year, the King's forces invaded Scotland. In 1640, the Long Parliament convened. The Parliamen-tarians, in their war of destiny with the King, were on the lookout for propagandists as well as pugilists with arms.

On this timeline, pamphleteering erupted on a scale unprecedented anywhere in the world.

The pamphleteer Milton emerges as anti-Episcopalian; that is, a bishop-basher or a wrecker of bishops. As such, he was attracted to Presbyterianism (he would not have made much of a Puritan). A product, among other influences, of the Calvinist Reformation in Scotland, this is a form of church governance through councils, with representatives drawn from the congregation, a feature of which is the distinct absence of bishops. Milton, being Milton, sees in this structure of governance a reflection of the ancient Athenian model. The debut pamphlet *Prelatical Episcopacy* of 1641 argued for the reform of Church governance. The bishops, Milton protested, governed church affairs for their advantage, and stood (bloated by good living) between the people and the reformed Church of England; an argument that, of course, played into the hands of the manic Puritan tendency. In his prose, Milton eviscerates his targets, with a narrative pendulum that swings between cruelty and hilarity. If Milton was trying to draw attention to himself as much as his subject matter, he succeeded. The bishops were at first surprised by the effrontery, and then outraged. A flurry of pamphlets, five in all, followed that same year on the same theme: *Of Reformation touching Church discipline*, among them. In the tradition of pamphleteering, a tortuous or bizarre title is irresistible, as with *An apology against a Pamphlet called a Modest Confutation of the Anim-adversions* (also 1641). As a pamphleteer, Milton rema-ined detached, with an esoteric cast of mind, but he was *un*worldly; he needed experience, not of books, but of a life *lived* rather than thought about or observed. This invited domesticity (a kind of hell for Milton), which is surely not the same thing as worldly affairs, and so the epic poetry would have to wait a good while yet. In a sense, Milton seems to have *waited* his entire life · even for *Paradise Lost*, which, unusually for a poet, he produced late in life.

In August 1642, the English Civil War unleashed forces beyond any ordinary understanding (which might also be said of Milton's first marriage). In 1643, as the conflict mounted, Milton took unto himself a wife: Mary Powell. She was only seventeen to his thirty-four years. Why Mary? An infatuation, the irresistible novelty of it all, is the most probable reason. Pure folly is another reason. The lofty-minded Milton seems to have misunderstood (he is not alone there) or even despised women in general. In the present era, there are those who would brand him a *misogynist*. As Milton married three times, he must have been a glutton for this special kind of punishment. His view of the female seemed to be that of a convenient but unrealistic hybrid of guardian angel and domestic slave. Mary, his youthful wife, was neither. In the early weeks of the marriage, she deserted her husband. Milton never quite got over this.

When Cromwell came to power, Mary pleaded forgiveness. The Powells were Royalist, and had fallen on hard times. She returned, bore Milton three daughters, and died aged only twenty-seven. As for Milton, the aloof father, even his daughters hated him; this was, of course, entirely his own fault. Such was his nature: he remained remote, beyond reach. Then again, there were always other, greater matters to consider.

As the Civil War tore the country apart, these were perilous times to engage with pamphleteering. Milton, though, was set on making a name for himself, if not yet as a poet, then to continue as a writer of controversial tracts. After the separation from his first wife, the academic in Milton sparked: now, he had some real-life material to hand. John Milton, poet in abeyance, once again took up his pen as pamphleteer on the national stage. His subject matter? Divorce, the Civil War - all, in Milton's mind, somehow interwoven.

So by 1643, the year of his very brief marriage, Milton had turned to the subject of marital breakdown with the pamphlet *The Doctrine and Discipline of Divorce*, which found a much wider, especially interested audience. Since marriage was, and is, bestowed as a sacrament by the old church (usually by the reformed high church; often by the broad church), divorce was a highly controversial matter, with a social stigma (and remained so until recent decades). The principles espoused in the tract are well argued. The scrivener's son, unlike most poets, reveals a legal slant of mind. Milton would have made for an outstanding advocate, with his rapier-like mind. The motive for these pamphlets is, however, highly suspect as the author divests himself of his views and deliberations. In the way of many pamphleteers, there is another subject: *the author*, who occasionally slips (intentionally) into vulgar autobiography. The unwary reader of these tracts is drawn into a trap, cunningly devised by Milton, where the subject turns on the author's own persona, and fuses with the main narrative. As an attention-seeker, Milton is writing propaganda for himself in the guise of exploring greater themes. In this way, an unknown man is now famous. As an outcome, he came to the attention of other famous men, enemies and allies both, and one man among men in particular.

There was a hefty price to pay for this strategy, since Milton did not become known as a poet in his own country until he was an old man. In Florence, where he was already highly regarded, his admirers would not have

understood why this precocious English poet was wasting
his time, energies and talents on pamphlets. Milton
understood his English audience, though: that he would
not be read until he was famous or at least controversial.

The prose of these pamphlets, albeit effortless and
technically impressive, is heavy handed; and absent is the
deft hand of the poet. If anything, there are signs of a
brilliant scrivener at work. Otherwise, Milton is
essentially marking time until he finds some higher goal.
Again, Milton always seemed to be preparing himself for
some future project of an unspecified nature. As powerful
forces coursed across the land, the pamphlets served as a
training ground · for a singular pamphlet of universal
distinction: *Areopagitica. . .A Speech for Liberty of
Unlicensed Printing to the Parliament of England* (1644).
Milton is not so much 'speaking' about the free press, or
freedom of expression, but the *freedom of thought*. The
tract is a natural extension of his battle with the bishops.
Why allow this self-appointed elite to do all the thinking?
In Milton's day, the right to free expression was available
to anyone who was prepared to pay for the privilege, with
imprisonment, or with termination at the end of a rope.
The *Areopagitica* · the free press · is futuristic in its
intent, but its source is ancient. Who, though, was *he* to
lecture the powers of the land? As ever, Milton was no one
else but himself; and he viewed this self in the Athenian
mould. *Areopagitica* of the title is a speech to Parliament,
which Milton had no intention of delivering orally, and is
named for the legendary hill in Athens, the Areopagus, an
ancient platform of debate. On the front cover of the
pamphlet, he quotes Euripides:

> This is true Liberty when free born men
> Having to advise the public may speak free,
> Which he who can, and will, deserv's high praise,
> Who neither can nor will, may hold his peace;
> What can be juster in a State than this?

If Milton is lecturing Parliament, he was also defying, head-on, the recently enacted censorship law, and quoting ancient precedent (Isocrates, St. Paul, *et. al.*) in so doing. After the execution of Charles I, the greatly feared and thus despised Court of the Star Chamber had been abolished, which unleashed a wave of unlicensed printing. The Stationers' Company, with its vested interest much at stake, lobbied Parliament for action, and the Printing Ordinance of 1643 passed into law. The *Areopagitica* · as a plea for the 'free press' · is Milton's reply, and in which he argues, not for free expression, but for *status quo ante* or "the way things were before" or "the state that existed previously". In this context, censorship of pamphlets should, he argued, be applied where deemed necessary *after*, not *prior* to, publication, which is exactly the risk he took with the printing of the unlicensed *Areopagitica*. Although a supporter of Parliament (boosted by the victory of Marston Moor), Milton is prepared to lecture the honourable members as though they were an Athenian assembly, thus:

> For books are not absolutely dead things, but do
> contain a potency of life in them to be as active as
> that soul was whose progeny they are; nay, they do
> preserve as in a vial the purest efficacy and
> extraction of that living intellect that bred them.

And again, thus:

> And yet, on the other hand, unless wariness be
> used, as good almost kill a man as kill a good book.
> Who kills a man kills a reasonable creature, God's
> image; but he who destroys a good book, kills reason
> itself, kills the image of God, as it were in the eye. . .

The impact of the pamphlet: profound, and far-reaching. There is, of course, much more to the pamphlet than 'the press' and free expression; there is a powerful sense that what might now be called the *human condition* is up for discussion. Who else could have pulled this off but for the scrivener's son from Bread Street? Milton was on his way. In the event, the tract served as a highly eloquent general job application for its author. The most powerful men in the land now recognised that Milton might prove useful in the war of ideas. The fixers of the Cromwell regime set out to harness the propaganda value inherent in such outpourings. How might, for instance, a regicide be reconciled with a higher purpose? This had to be explained, and promptly. A poet, then, had his uses, after all; not for poetry just yet, but for pro-regime tracts - something, then, *useful* as with propaganda (which, or course, is exactly what Milton was doing for *himself* while he was at it).

In 1649, Milton was appointed Latin Secretary or Secretary of Foreign Tongues, which meant he became chief apologist for the regime in the arena of international relations. Outside, looking in, the English had done the unthinkable, and chopped-off the head of their anointed King. The reaction throughout the Royal Courts of Europe had been that of astonishment, then horror, that such a *wicked* precedent had been set. Where would it all end? Milton's task was to placate England's nervous allies in the near abroad.

This Milton accomplished, with spectacular zeal, and in doing so at last found his own self. Milton had for a while acted as a private tutor, but now he had a 'proper job' with a 'proper salary'. Again, the poetry would have to wait.

In the early years of the Interregnum, Milton had been a great admirer of Oliver Cromwell, whose vaulting ambition, moving along some parallel track, seemed to mirror that of the poet in waiting. As Milton matured, this view was to change; there had, to this refined mind, been something thuggish about the Cambridge squire, who was found to be vain and fallible as he underwent the transformation from plain-living man to Lord Protector. Now, it is difficult to imagine the two of them, Cromwell and Milton, seated together as the ruling Council of State deliberated (and Milton without a vote) amid the flickering candlelight.

If Marchmont Nedham had been the editor-in-chief for the Commonwealth with his monopoly 'news book' *Mercurius Politicus* (1650-60), then so too was Milton as pamphleteer-in-chief with such tracts as *The Tenure of Kings and Magistrates* (1649) and *The Readie and Easie Way to Establish a Free Commonwealth* (1660). This latter pamphlet appeared just after the death of Cromwell, with that inadequate son Richard in the ascendant. There was talk now of restoring the monarchy. In this interval, there were those who (though not Milton) looked outside of England's narrow, unsettled pastures to view the prospective Charles II in exile.

As a famous pamphleteer so closely associated with the Cromwell regime, he somehow survived the Restoration of 1661 under Charles II, who may have flinched from hanging in this most particular case. A final judgement on John Milton (who believed in Resurrection of body and soul) seems to have been suspended. The Latin Secretary's employment was terminated. Parliament issued an order for Milton's arrest, and the Sergeant-at-Arms detained him for period. The prospect of a show trial receded, and he escaped punishment. On payment of £150 in 'fees' (which he bitterly resented), Milton was released. Where some of the regicides had escaped into exile, others were tracked down, captured, disembowelled, and hanged. Someone, somewhere, appears to have intervened (the name Andrew Marvell is whispered here) on Milton's behalf. A most hideous execution had been deftly side-stepped. Milton suffered the mere indignity of certain of his books and pamphlets being incinerated. Eyesight failing rapidly, Milton took himself off to Bunhill Fields. Soon, as with his old acquaintance Galileo, he had joined the exclusive company of blind men. People were inclined to say that God had struck Milton blind - - for his part in the regime. And yet, he did not abide in the darkness. Milton's blindness was of a luminous kind, an opaque white un-seeingness, and a kind of purgatory. In this state, he dictated the epic poems. The voice of the poems is not so much Milton's as that of an elevated narrator. Who might that omniscient narrator be? Who else?

In 1674, the end came: John Milton, who was by then a famous man, died of 'gout stuck in'. The world has forgotten the pamphleteering, and remembered, for now, the epic poems; and Eden, where the Milton's serpent forever tempts Eve to tempt Adam. John Milton is buried at St. Giles of Cripplegate in London, alongside another John Milton: the scrivener, his father. The last words here, though, are left, not with the elevated narrator, but with those attributed to a fellow poet: "This man has left us all behind."

Fig. 17 John Milton (1608-1674): a formidabl character; imperious, lofty-minded. As Lati Secretary with the Cromwell regime, Milto proved deft at paperwork and foreign tongue. After the execution of Charles I, Milto functioned as chief propagandist for the regim and was infamous long before he became know as a famous poe

Milton narrowly escaped the gallows of th Restoration to dictate, in his blind old ag *Paradise Lost* (1672

Fig. 18 *Areopagitica* (1644): written as a speech to Parliament, which, of course, Milton had no intention of delivering. In 1641, the Puritan-dominated Parliament had abolished the Star Chamber court of Charles I, which provoked a rash of unlicensed printing. The Stationers' Company petitioned Parliament, and the House enacted the Printing Ordinance of 1643 to control 'the press'.

The *Areopagitica* is Milton's response, and the greatest plea ever for free expression, which for Milton meant freedom of thought.

The tract is named for a hill in Athens, "Areopagus", a legendary site of ancient debate. In the *Areopagitica*, the pamphlet had come of age.

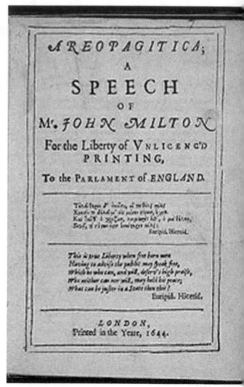

Daniel Defoe
at the Coffee House

DANIEL DEFOE appears to have been no one but himself, although there are visible transformations of that same self in a career as merchant, financial speculator, subversive pamphleteer, government spy and propa-gandist, pioneer editor and journalist of his "News Paper" the *Review*, and eventually world famous novelist of *Robinson Crusoe* and *Moll Flanders*. The thread of Daniel Defoe's life is aligned, and so informed by, some of the most extraordinary events in British history and in Europe, which presage the birth of the periodical press.

Daniel Foe (the sophistication of 'De' was added later) was born to James and Alice Foe in 1660·1661? on the eve of the Restoration. The Foe family were most likely residents of the parish of St. Giles in London's Cripplegate. James Foe was a tallow merchant and a member of The Butcher's Company. The family were Dissenters, so called, or non-conformists (that is, any Protestant who stood apart from the established Church of England), and this determined much of the pattern of the boy Daniel's life. As a Presbyterian, he attended the Dissenters' Academy at Stoke Newington (overseen by Charles Morton, later a vice president at Harvard University). The Academy provided an eclectic education, where a boy's curiosity, and perhaps even the imagination, might be stimulated. This was, though, the end of the academic road for Defoe · or indeed anyone else who was a non-conformist. This had all been very well in Cromwell's day, but after the Restoration those labelled as Dissenters were subject to prejudice and generally treated with suspicion. For the rest of his life, then, Defoe remained an outsider; even, later on, in Grub Street (today, Ropemaker's Street), which in its way was an early precursor to Fleet Street. On leaving school, his options were strictly limited. Any kind of social ambition towards class status (as with the likes of Swift, Addison and Steele, who lived on a different plane of reality) was (really) out of the question. The avenues of advancement for the attainment of social rank (craved for in those days; misunderstood now, and displaced by a sense of entitlement) were closed-off by the iron curtain of social exclusion. In his family's denomination, he might have chosen the path of minister in the Presbyterian Church. Instead, he entered the City of London in 1681 as a merchant; and, soon enough, financial mis-adventurer. As a hosier factor or merchant, Defoe concerned himself with all to do with stockings (this is not *lingerie*); that is, mostly woollen leggings of all kinds; and he travelled across England in search of reliable supplies of wool (and, no doubt, absorbing the materiál for what would one day become his travelogue *Tour of Great Britain*).

In 1684, he married a wealthy cooper's daughter, Mary Tuffley. Of the cooper's daughter and the barrel-maker's craft, Defoe learned much - and received much. A dowry of £3,700 sweetened the honeymoon.

Defoe was on his reckless (but certainly not feckless) way. First, a horse, and with his own horse, this newly married man seems to have participated in the Battle of Sedgemore (1685), which defeated the Duke of Monmouth's Rebellion against his uncle James II (brother of Charles II). On the losing side, Defoe survived Sedgemore as a fugitive who faced the bloody assizes of the hanging Judge Jeffreys. Events soon turned: somehow Defoe's name came to be included in a general pardon, and so he lived to see the eventual overthrow of the Catholic James II and the Glorious Revolution of 1688.

The Parliamentary *coup de grâce* of the Glorious Revolution (1689) has almost been erased from the minds of inhabitants of the British Isles today, with the exception, perhaps, of the north of Ireland, where Jacobite forces were finally defeated at the Battle of the Boyne (1690). The Glorious Revolution ensured the Protestant Succession in England: William of Orange was installed on the throne of England as William III with the balancing act of Mary Stuart as his Queen. These were extraordinary times of national trans-formation and realignment to build the permanent way ahead. The English Parliament, free of Stuart absolutism, assumed powers to raise serious capital. The instruments were the creation of the National Debt leading to the establishment of the Bank of England (Royal Charter 1694) by Charles Montague. The South Sea Company was founded in 1711 by Robert Harley (q.v.) and the speculative South Sea Bubble was on its way (and in which Defoe was to exert an early influence).

Outside of the hosiery business, Defoe was also inclined to speculative financial misadventure and outlandish schemes for self-enrichment: musk from cat glands for perfume-making; a diving bell investment for the recovery of sunken treasure, etc., etc. As a pamphleteer in the making, probably the most prolific ever, his résumé is no less than superb as a man of affairs.

As a regular of the coffee houses, Defoe was exposed to a torrent of vital information: shipping news from the world over, shipwreck, cargoes spoilt or lost, mutiny; commercial and low-grade intelligence; scandal, and gossip - all of this is "news". The coffee shops or houses were information exchanges, like a living, breathing 'newspaper' - a newsroom. Defoe must have revelled in these places as he rubbed shoulders with shipping agents, insurance brokers, intelligencers, financiers, and money-lenders. The wife's dowry? Don't ask. A small fortune in today's coin. There were some five hundred of these coffee shops in London alone at this time. In 1652, Pasque Rosee, a Greek, established the first of these in St. Michael's Alley, Cornhill. Edward Lloyd's coffee house, frequented by shipping under-writers, evolved into the still-extant newspaper *Lloyds List (est.* 1734). The London Stock Exchange grew out of a coffee house where stock and commodity prices were posted daily. In this way, many coffee shops had a specialist clientele - Whigs, Tories, adherents to various factions, literary types, wool merchants, up-market con-men, and so on. Defoe would have been a recognisable figure in many of these establishments and at various stages of his kaleidoscopic career. As such, Defoe had access to London's highly sophisticated financial community. So he borrowed to finance speculation, and again he borrowed more to service the debts incurred; and, it seems, he may not have been such a straightforward fellow with which to deal. In 1692, his creditors caught up with him: he was served with a class-action lawsuit for £17,000, a huge sum at the time, and so he was bankrupted. That meant disgrace, and prison at the Fleet until some deal could be worked out. Three months passed, after which he had agreed a settlement of sorts with his creditors.

ONCE SET FREE, the jailbird Defoe looked east to Tilbury, where he owned a parcel of land that had somehow escaped the clutches of his creditors. On this site (possibly with help from King William), he established a brickworks, a *sensible* venture, which also turned out pantiles or *S*-shaped roof tiles. An innovative geometric design from the Continent eliminated the need for mortar. In London, the demand was vast. Soon, Defoe had cleared most of his debts, and he acquired a fine house in Stoke Newington. The bankruptcy and the lost dowry rankled yet, but now he was a man of property and business, with a wife and children.

Then, in 1701, he was diverted into yet another activity, with his first *known* outing as a pamphleteer. The focus of the subject matter was William of Orange. A King of England, who was not English, for many people at this time, was better than even the prospect of an English king who was a Catholic - anything but that (and this still holds today). A Dutchman, and the Stadtholder of the United Provinces of Holland, William was not much interested in England - or Ireland - except as a power base as the leader of Protestant Europe in the Grand Alliance that stood against the European superpower of day: the France of Louis XIV (the Sun King), as the War of the Spanish Succession loomed over the horizon. A man like Daniel Defoe (a confidant of "King Billy", so it would seem) had his uses. As propagandist, Defoe's satirical verse pamphlet *A True-Born Englishman* (1701) defended William against accusations of those among the English who saw an ill-mannered foreigner, *etc., etc.,* on the throne. (The tract seems a rather belated defence of King William, who passed away in 1702.) As Defoe's most famous pamphlet, the verse tract suggested that there was no such being as real Englishman, since all came from elsewhere - *foreigners all*. Defoe possesses an easy style and the common touch; although cast in verse, the words are deft, light hearted - and so Defoe captured the hearts of a wide enough audience.

The opening lines remain strangely familiar:

Wherever God erects a house of prayer
The Devil always builds a chapel there;
And 't will be found, upon examination
The latter has the largest congregation.

The pamphlet was hugely popular, with forty editions in all. Defoe's name had been made. The wool merchant turned brick-maker was on his way as a pamphleteer and propagandist. For William, though, time was running out as he approached the end of his reign and his exhausting life. As the seventeenth gave way to the eighteenth century, the tumultuous reign of Queen Anne was about to begin.

In these years, Defoe's output was prolific, and wide ranging in its subject matter. In all, over two hundred pamphlets have been attributed to his name. As such, he asserted primacy as a man of the press. Among England's earliest professional journalists, Defoe is innovative - for instance - in the arena of political economy, and produced such tracts as *An Essay upon Projects* (1697) and *Proposals for Employing the Poor in and about the City of London without any charge to the Publick* (1700). In a vision worthy of Robinson Crusoe, he also wrote *An Essay on the South Sea Trade,* which appears to have had some influence on the formation of the South Sea Company that eventually led to the ruinous financial disaster known as the South Sea Bubble. Defoe had made his name, but now he had much to lose. By 1703, his next pamphlet was about to explode in his face in the way of an incendiary device.

In an infamous sermon of the day, a certain Dr Sacheverell had spoken out against Dissenters, who, the good doctor asserted, most wilfully stood apart from the Church of England. Defoe found that he was unable to resist a counterblast, which also proved to be his undoing.

The Shortest Way with Dissenters (1703) was intended as a hoax, but the tract was not received as such by the authorities, who were not - and *are* not, necessarily - of a satirical bent of mind. The pamphlet, instead of attacking the sourpuss Sacheverell's views, accepted and stretched these views to the extreme. *The Shortest Way* was, as it were, at the end of rope: hang the lot of them. The tract made fools out of the good doctor and his disciples. There were many high Tory churchmen, though, who were inclined to agree with the outrageous proposals of *The Shortest Way*, not at first realising that the anonymous author was himself a Dissenter. These were very serious people, who are always ready to be fooled, and so Defoe had made fools out of them: the authorities. They had been had. This was Defoe's real crime.

Defoe was promptly arrested and cross-examined. The only known portrait of Defoe is based on a vague description of him at the time of the arrest. On 7 July 1703, he stood trial, and pleaded guilty to the charge of seditious pamphleteering. As Defoe stood in the dock, he must have studied the faces of the judges, some of the very same men he had lampooned. The judgement was severe indeed: he was fined, sent to the pillory for three days, and sentenced to confinement for an indeterminate term. Apocryphal, perhaps, but while Defoe stood in the pillory, the crowd - instead of throwing the customary missiles - is said to have showered Defoe with flowers. Defoe marked the occasion with the pamphlet *Hymn to the Pillory*, a pamphlet-poem in which he cast himself in the role of victim: the judges should be stood in pillory, not himself, *etc., etc.* Somehow, the pamphlet was on sale at the event. Flowers or stones, whichever, his next stop was "Newgate Prison's cold embrace," as he described that place.

The experience of incarceration seems to have transformed Defoe, with his exaggerated sense of being an
outsider on the inside; and at Newgate he was very much
on the *inside*. In prison, there was plenty of time to reflect.
What had possessed Defoe to produce *The Shortest Way*?
Queen Anne wanted to know, but she could not elicit a
convincing reason as to his motive. Did he, Her Majesty
wondered, have accomplices?

The licensing of pamphlets had effectively lapsed back
in 1695, but this was surely not an open invitation to
lampoon the authorities with subversive pamphlets. In
prison, an idea came to him by way of a dream: a "News
Paper". The dream would spur Defoe into journalism, not
as visionary of the free press, or a seeker of truth, but out
of sheer desperation. (This is as good a reason as any.)
Defoe, though, was still on the inside.

On the outside, there were those in high places who had
recognised Defoe's potential as a propagandist in the
service of the state. Robert Harley was a principal minister
in the government of the day, and for a time First Minister
to Queen Anne. Harley would soon survive an assassination attempt, which would boost his popularity and see
him ennobled as the Earl of Oxford. Harley was among the
first of those politicians to realise the power of 'the press'
over censorship, and Defoe the outsider was a likely
candidate for grooming as a government spy and
propagandist. How long, though, had he languished in
Newgate? Four months of an indeterminate sentence at
the Queen's pleasure was long enough. The invisible hand
of Robert Harley cast its spell (with a wan smile from Her
Majesty, who paid his fine) and Defoe was released in early
November of 1703.

AN EMBITTERED JAILBIRD, Defoe re-joined his family. He
wrote to Harley (as Harley had anticipated) with words of
gratitude in all humility for the intervention. Since the
Tilbury brickworks had been ruined, he now turned, not to
dangerous pamphleteering, but to journalism. Only a few
weeks after his release from prison, Nature provided him
with an opportunity. On the 25 November 1703, the Great
Storm struck the British Isles with hurricane force. The
devastation was awesome in its scale. Over 8,000 people
are thought to have lost their lives on land and at sea.
Defoe recorded: ". . .the bricks, tiles and stones from the
tops of houses flew with such force, and so thick in the
streets, that no one thought fit to venture out, though their
houses were near demolished within."

There is a supreme irony here: had his Tilbury
brickworks remained operational, he might well have
made a great fortune supplying London with vast supplies
of replacement pantiles. Instead, as editor-in-chief and
lead writer, he acted as a one-man newsroom: Defoe's
notice in the *London Gazette* appealed for eyewitness
accounts from across the country. A kind of reporting by
remote observation, he collated and editorialised the
diverse submissions to produce an account of history in the
making: *The Storm: or a Collection of the most
Remarkable Disasters which Happened in the late
dreadful Tempest both by Sea and Land.*

Robert Harley, though, had not sprung Defoe from
prison to write about extremes of weather.

By 1704, Defoe had been prompted to act on the
Newgate dream, with the launch of his "News Paper", this
being *Review of the Affairs of France.* The weekly, then
thrice-weekly, four-pager was produced almost entirely by
Defoe. Government agents bought-up copies to boost

circulation. Before long, Defoe was the most influential journalist in England, with regular visits to the coffee shops, where the newspaper was made available to the clientele (for a mere a penny, then an ha'penny, per issue).

In this way, the coffee shops were both newsrooms and newsagents, with Defoe as go-between and editor of a stable of periodicals, the *Review* among them. Far ahead of the Grub Street 'hacks', Defoe came up with such innovations as the bogus Letter to the Editor (which he usually wrote himself). The habitués of Grub Street could not abide Defoe, but he was (under the terms of his release from prison) prohibited from responding to their insults. "You Dog, you," one correspondent concluded a letter, which Defoe faithfully reproduced. As a "News Paper" the *Review* provided a form of commentary as propaganda, since the periodical, albeit with some diversions, tended to promote the government's (*i.e.,* the Harley Ministry's) policies at home and abroad.

At home, Robert Harley had a special project for Defoe: preparing the way for the Union of Scotland and England, no less, which the *Review* promoted (in spite of its full title...*of the Affairs of France*) to sway public opinion in favour of the Act of Union (in 1707). In 1706, Harley even went so far as to send Defoe on a secret mission to Edinburgh as a government spy, this to determine the mood 'on the ground', with frequent field reports sent back to London. As Defoe exerted influence as lobbyist in favour of the Treaty, the risk of discovery as an English spy in Scotland might have had fatal consequences for Defoe, but for Harley the stakes were much higher than the life of a mere undercover journalist.

Abroad, the stakes were much higher yet again. In the War of the Spanish Succession (1701-1714), Louis XIV of

France had Bourbon dynastic ambitions on the throne of Spain, which England and her allies were determined to block. The enfeebled Charles II of Spain (*reign* 1665-1700) had named Louis' grandson, Philippe duc d'Ajour, as his successor. England's preferred candidate was *not* the Bourbon heir apparent; instead, England looked to the Habsburg pretender or heir presumptive, the Archduke of Austria, who waited in the wings as would-be Charles III of Spain. The pan-European stand-off, which also had far-reaching consequences overseas, unleashed the clash between the royal houses of Bourbon and Habsburg.

In England, the support of public opinion was vital as the Duke of Marlborough pursued his grand Mediterranean strategy (devised by the late King William)). In 1704, the same year the *Review* was launched, Marlborough achieved a great victory at Blenheim, and Britain captured Gibraltar from Spain (on behalf, said Queen Anne, of the Habsburg Archduke of Austria, the prospective Charles III of Spain.

Defoe continued with the newspaper on 'foreign affairs' (among matters closer to home) until the signing of the Treaty of Utrecht (1713). This was the pan-European settlement of its day based on the balance of power negotiated between Great Britain, Spain, France, Savoy, and the United Provinces (the Dutch Republic). France and Spain agreed to remain as separate realms under two crowns. Philippe, the duc d'Anjou, grandson of Louis XIV (as Charles II had intended) was eventually recognized as Felipe V, King of Spain (already anointed as such since 1700), the first Bourbon King of that realm (*reign* 1700-1724; 1724-1746). Under the Treaty, Spain's European possessions were divided: the Spanish Netherlands (Belgium today) went to Charles VI, Holy Roman Emperor (one and the same Charles, Archduke of Austria, *etc., etc.*); Spain ceded Gibraltar to Britain "in perpetuity" (Article X); and, beyond Europe, Portugal's possessions in Brazil were recognised, and so on, & *etc.* Then, after so many lives expended, England withdrew from the European conflict, which continued among the remaining adversaries until the Treaty of Rastadt in 1714.

For Defoe, his days as an influential journalist were coming to an end. In that same year, with the passing of Queen Anne, Robert Harley and the Tories fell from office, and the long years of the Georgian era stretched out ahead. In this period, Defoe may have performed services for the incoming Whig government, and there is some evidence that he may have re-entered the world of financial speculation. In these years, too, Defoe is a pamphleteer unbound, with a curiosity and energy undiminished as he unleashed a fresh wave of tracts, among them: *Minutes of the Negotiations of M. Mesnager* (1717), which mimics the French diplomat who negotiated the Treaty of Utrecht; *A Political History of the Devil* (1726) and *A System of Magic* (1726).

By this time, Defoe had already embarked on a parallel career as the ambitious author of fictions based often on solid enough reality. In *The Journal of a Plague Year* (1722), he found a high level of sophistication with its realism, and for which he remains a key figure in the development of English prose. As an 'eyewitness' account, though, the author writes retrospectively of events that occurred when he was only six-years-old; but he convinces with an eye for detail and a highly original talent for narrative.

Then Defoe outclassed himself: with an account of that other island: *A Tour Thro' the Whole Island of Great*

Britain (1724-25), a three-volume survey of pre-industrial Britain. *The Tour* is regarded by many scholars as Defoe's outstanding achievement. As the author of these works, he was an innovator whose legacy remains impressive, even after the passing of almost three centuries. From the coffee house to prison, and back again, the locus of Daniel Defoe's extraordinary life found its final exit-point. . .he walked out of his house, abandoned his family, and then vanished into the bowels of London. The creditors, no doubt, were in hot pursuit of the famous novelist until the end. As in life, intrigue pursued Defoe into the ground. In 1731, Defoe died a fugitive. Beyond the reach of his creditors forever, his remains were buried at Bunhill Field Cemetery in London. Mary Defoe died the following year. In 1871, when the grave was opened to erect the present monument ("Paid for by the schoolchildren of London"), Mary Defoe's remains were discovered interred along-side those of her husband. A third coffin was unearthed, that of a female (perhaps one of their children). The epitaph reads:

Daniel De-Foe

1661 - 1731

Author of Robinson Crusoe

The name of Daniel Defoe is forever associated with the castaway *Robinson Crusoe* (1719) and the orange-seller *Moll Flanders* (1722), both of whom cast longer shadows than even their creator. There is more, though, to *Robinson Crusoe* (which most readers of the day took as a real-life account of shipwreck and maroon), than the story of a castaway who sees a footprint in the sand that is not his own.

Coda

DANIEL DEFOE had created "Man as single-handed antagonist of Nature," as has been said, which in this present day has taken on a global dimension. As for that other castaway, Jonathan Swift's Gulliver's Travels appeared in 1726. The dates here are intriguing: since Swift took about seven years to write Gulliver, the Dean must have embarked on his epic task on the very first appearance of Crusoe. In its fundamental dimensions, Gulliver clearly parodies in a parallax view Defoe's marooned Crusoe, though at a much higher level of sophistication than its putative source: but Defoe got his castaway afloat first, and without Robinson Crusoe there might well have been no Lemuel Gulliver; although Swift is, in a sense, making a parody of all tales of voyages to remote regions, shipwreck, and castaways on strange shores. The primary source for Crusoe is usually cited as Alexander Selkirk's misadventure; the sources, though, are nebulous, with such as William Dampier's New Voyage round the World (1697), which had a profound influence on Europeans of the day. If Gulliver is the literary son of Crusoe, then this also reflects the rivalry between Defoe and Swift. The depiction of the human condition is divergent, with Crusoe's realism versus the fantastical satire of Gulliver; but, whichever, both these tales have been reduced to children's stories by a world distracted by the unexpected ennui of paradise and the unbelievable nature of the remote regions where horses talk and humans are nought but disgusting Yahoos. Defoe and Swift were both pamphleteers; as propagandists, both were in the service of Robert Harley, First Minister to Queen Anne. Any similarity between Defoe and Swift as men or men of letters ends there. Defoe was human in his wayward vices, a risk-taker, and prone to misfortune.

Jonathan Swift was something else entirely.

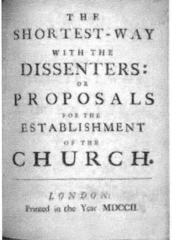

Fig. 19 Daniel Defoe (1660-1731): earlier in his career, the author of *Robinson Crusoe* had been a hosier (stockings) merchant, pamphleteer, and influential journalist.

Image: Michael van de Gucht (1706) line engraving after Jeremiah Taverner's construed portrait is based on a vague description at the time of Defoe's arrest. In 1703, his downfall came when his anonymous satirical pamphlet backfired...

Fig. 20 *The Shortest-Way with Dissenters* (1703): the pamphlet exploded in Defoe's face. The tract was a hoax, but the judges at his trial did not see it that way: he was fined, pilloried, and imprisoned at Newgate. Robert Harley, First Minister to Queen Anne, arranged for Defoe's release, then put him to work as government propagandist and spy.

Fig. 21 De Foe in the Pillory: The story goes (apocryphal, no doubt) that instead of being pelted with the customary missiles, Defoe's pamphlet *Hymn to the Pillory* inspired the mob to shower the prisoner with flowers. *Painting:* ***De Foe in the Pillory*** (1862): long after the event, Sir Eyre Crowe imagined the scene, *with* the flowers. *Courtesy*: *National Portrait Gallery, London.*

PROPOSALS

For Imploying the

POOR

In and about the

CITY of *London,*

Without any CHARGE to
the PUBLICK.

LONDON,

Printed for *J. Baker* at the *Black-Boy* in
Pater-noster-Row. M.DCC.XIII.

Price Three Pence.

Fig. 22 *Proposals for Employing the Poor* (1713) *attrib.* to D. Defoe: this and such pamphlets as *An Essay on Projects* (1697) reveal Defoe as a pioneer of an advanced form of journalism on what today would be termed 'political economy'.

Fig. 23 A Coffee House in the Queen Anne era of the kind frequented by Defoe. The coffee houses were the 'news rooms' of London (shipping, insurance, *etc.*), where periodicals were made available to patrons. After 1695, the relaxation of censorship and the explosive growth in the number of coffee shops (over 500 in London alone) opened the way for the emergence of the periodical press at the turn of the eighteenth century.

Among these, Defoe's *Review* (1704-1713) promoted the Union of Scotland and England (1707) and Marlborough's campaign in the War of the Spanish Succession (1701-1714). The idea for a "News Paper" came to Defoe in a dream while in prison.

Fig. 24 Jonathan Swift (1667-1745): Dean of Saint Patrick's, Dublin, and the greatest satirist of the age. In the interval between *Tale of a Tub* (1704) and *Gulliver's Travels* (1726), the clergyman had been a highly influential and even notorious pamphleteer. Painting: Charles Jervas (c. 1718). *Courtesy: National Portrait Gallery, London.*

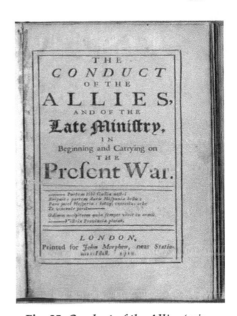

Fig. 25 *Conduct of the Allies* (*orig.* 1711; 1712 *ed. shown*): albeit propaganda, Swift's masterful, 25,000-word account of the conflict with Louis XIV of France sold 11,000 copies and was quoted in Parliament. The tract undermined Marlborough's campaign in Europe and promoted the Tory plan for peace ahead of the Treaty of Utrecht (1713).

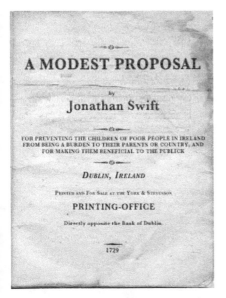

Fig. 26 *A Modest Proposal* (*orig.*1724; 1729 *ed. shown*) is the only publication by the Dean to bear his name. A masterpiece of sustained irony, the tract ridicules the wealthy landowners of Ireland, who appeared quite indifferent to the human degradations surrounding their grand estates. The poor, he observed, had one resource in abundance that might be used for mutual benefit.

The Remote Regions *of*
Jonathan Swift

THE ORIGINATOR of *Tale of a Tub* (1704) and the masterpiece *Gulliver's Travels* (1726) was a churchman who spent his life in search of preferment within the establishment, while inclining to ridicule the human condition and society. Except for a single pamphlet, his output was anonymous; then again, the Dean's imprint was unmistakable for those in the know.

The greatest satirist of the age, and perhaps of any age, Jonathan Swift was born in Dublin of Anglo-Irish parentage on 30 November 1667. By the time of his birth, his father Jonathan had already died (cause unknown), and soon after his mother Abigail moved to England, without him. The boy and his sister Jane grew up at No. 7 Hoey's Court (no longer standing), where relatives on the father's side of the family raised them. In later life, the Dean looked back on his childhood years, and wrote that he had grown up "like a dog" - an allusion, no doubt, to his lowly status as kind of house animal, with a dead father, an absent mother, and a burden perhaps on his relatives.

The 1673, the young Swift left the Hoey's Court household to join Kilkenny College as a border. In 1682, he went on to Trinity College, Dublin, where he gained a BA in 1686. An already unsettled student, Swift's MA studies were interrupted in 1689 by the great changes taking place in the outside world. This is the era of the Glorious Revolution, with the accession of William of Orange to the throne of England as William III, and the decisive defeat of Jacobite forces at the Battle of the Boyne in 1690. The change of regime favoured those so placed. In England, long established Anglo-Irish family relations allowed for Swift's relocation to Moor Park in Surrey as a private secretary to Sir William Temple. A retired diplomat of high distinction, Sir William had negotiated the Triple Alliance (England, Sweden, United Provinces) of 1668 as a bulwark against King Louis XIV of France, and as such was a long-standing confidant of King William. In this respect, Swift found himself, for one so young, in a highly unusual position. As Sir William gained confidence in his private secretary, Swift undertook special assignments as a courier or go-between for the highly influential Temple circle.

At Moor Park, Swift first encountered Esther Johnson (then an eight-year-old), the putative daughter of a woman servant - and supposedly fatherless. She bore a striking resemblance - even for those too polite to notice - to the head of the household: Sir William. Swift, who was related to Sir William, was then most probably a blood relative of Esther (his secret name for her was "Stella"), and he maintained a deep, albeit unusual, friendship with Esther until the end of her days.

In 1690, Swift experienced fits of giddiness. In this state of poor health, he left Moor Park and returned to Ireland. The occasions of vertigo (now known as Ménière's syndrome) would remain with him for life. After a spell, he returned to England, and once again headed for Moor Park. In the interval of his second stay with Sir William, Swift gained an MA from Oxford in 1692. After a time, he seems to have become disillusioned with any prospect of advancement under Sir William's patronage. In 1694, he was ordained, and once again he left Moor Park, then to serve as vicar in the distant parish of Kilroot, near Belfast. There seems to have been a passing courtship with a "Varina" - a certain Miss Jane Waring.

After two years at this remote location, Swift returned for a third and final period in the service of Sir William. Once again, he proved himself unusually helpful to the master of the house. In 1697, Swift made his first attempt at satire with *The Battle of the Books* (pub. 1704), which defended Sir William's essay *Of Ancient and Modern Learning* (1690) against its many critics. The battle is between ancient and modern books, for which Swift chose the metaphors of a bee and a spider, and along the way indicated he thought the entire discussion as ludicrous. In any case, there can have been few private secretaries up to such a task. In those years, too, Swift also occupied himself with the formidable task of editing Sir William's memoirs and correspondence for publication, which would ultimately prove controversial. The Temple family considered that Swift as editor had been rather too indiscrete. As for Sir William, he was beyond caring when he died in January 1699. For Swift, not only had he lost a patron, he had also alienated the extended Temple family.

Swift left Moor Park for the last time, greatly more ambitious than when he had arrived. He returned to Ireland, where he took up the position of vicar at Laracor, about twenty miles from Dublin, in Country Meath. He also served as chaplain to Early of Berkeley (among the Lords Justice of Ireland). Esther or 'Stella', who was by then a young woman, also left Moor Park and travelled to Ireland; she wanted to be close by, but lived elsewhere to avoid any suspicion or taint of scandal. (There has been much speculation as to consanguinity - that is, the mixing of bloodlines between relatives - with the possibility of a secret marriage or love pact).

In 1702, the same year King William passed away, Swift acquired the degree of Doctor of Divinity from Trinity College, Dublin. Dr Swift (as he was now known) had his eyes fixed on advancement, and with a Laracor congregation of only fifteen souls he had time on his hands.

In 1704, he published *Tale of a Tub* with the earlier *The Battle of the Books* appearing (for the first time) in the same volume. By this time, Swift was a frequent visitor to England as a representative of the Church of Ireland. In London, he discovered he had won many admirers for the otherwise anonymous *Tale of a Tub*. The ingenious title derives from the maritime tradition of a ship's crew tossing empty barrels over-board to distract passing whales. The satire ridicules religious extremism, with an allegory of three brothers: Peter (Rome), Jack (non-conformist Protestant), and Martin (Lutheran). For good measure, the narrator adopts the persona of a resident of Bedlam.

Dr Swift of Dublin had made his mark. The famous author of *Tale of a Tub* had an unlikely profile for a provincial cleric with an obscure parish near Dublin. In London, he was a man of influence, with an insatiable appetite for church affairs, politics, and the literary life of the capital. Swift's primary mission, though, was on behalf of the Church of Ireland (and himself). He lobbied for "Queen Anne's Bounty" established in 1704, which gifted some £2,500 *per annum* to the clergy in England, but *not* to those in Ireland. In this aim, Queen Anne demurred, and Swift made next to no progress in this cause with the dominant Whigs. The opposition Tories (waiting like hawks in the wings) proved more tractable, since they already had their eyes on this especial cleric for reasons far removed from any Bounty.

In 1710, when Swift returned to London, the Tories were poised to regain power. In this period, too, he formed a liaison with a certain "Vanessa", which again was far from straightforward. The affair, if that is the right term for this remote liaison, was conducted in parallel with his long-standing friendship with "Stella".

As for "Vanessa", this was his codename for Hester Vanhomrigh, who also relocated to Dublin to be near Swift, unknown to "Esther" - or *vice versa*. For a clergyman, this remote *ménage à trois* was surely a complex arrangement.

In London again, Swift moved in exalted circles as a man of affairs on speaking terms with Robert Harley (soon to be Earl of Oxford) and Henry St. John (Lord Bolingbroke, prime candidate for Lemuel Gulliver). If there was scant progress in terms of preferment in the church, he had already made great strides within the London literary world since *Tale of a Tub*. Joseph Addison and Richard Steele invited Swift to contribute to the fledgling *The Tatler* (1709-11) and then *The Spectator* (1711-12). The format of *The Tatler* (although not so much the content of the essays) was clearly modelled after Defoe's *Review* (*c.*1704-13). Defoe usually had high praise his for his rivals Addison and Steele, but for "the scribbler" he reserved a special contempt, which was, of course, reciprocated. The reason was professional rivalry more than anything else. By 1710, Swift had been recruited by Robert Harley to edit the moderate Tory newspaper *The Examiner*. A literary man, Harley was far ahead of his rivals in understanding the value of propaganda, and as such he had once been a patron of Defoe. As a one-man "News Paper", Defoe's *Review* primarily covered the European campaign against Louis XIV of France in the War of the Spanish Succession. In 1708, when Harley was forced out of office, Defoe had continued with the *Review*. By 1710, Harley had defected to the Tories, and soon returned to office as Lord of the Treasury, effectively First Minister to Queen Anne.

In the interim, with the change of regime, Swift had

displaced Defoe as favoured propagandist.

In the European arena, the new Tory administration had contrived a secret plan for a grand settlement (involving illegal negotiations with France), which took a rather different view of Marlborough and his European campaign. In this purview, Jonathan Swift promoted the master plan with the pamphlet *Conduct of the Allies* (1711). From the allegorical satire of *Tale of a Tub*, Dr Swift had moved on to the elevated plane of international affairs with a 25,000-word assessment of the war in Europe: Louis XIV's offer of a peace deal in 1709-10 should have been accepted; Marlborough's campaign against Phillip of Spain was sheer folly, *etc., etc.* The blame for all of this was placed firmly on the outgoing Whig Ministry, which had brought the country to war and wrecked any prospect of peace.

In the *Review*, Daniel Defoe had been tracking the conflict since 1704, and so took against the analysis offered by his rival. There is no doubt, though, that Swift's masterful text, albeit party political propaganda for the Tories (with the outward goal of a European peace, and the inward aim of regime change at home) reaches a high pinnacle in the chronicles of the pamphleteers. The anonymous pamphlet, which sold in the region of 11,000 copies, was quoted in Parliament, and was instrumental in turning opinion against the Continental war, while defusing the Whig stance of "no peace with Spain".

The pamphlet, released in November 1711, also undermined the already damaged reputation of Marlborough; and Queen Anne, for reasons of her own, dismissed her commander-in-chief in the December of that year. The Whigs were out, the Tories were in: the new administration decided to negotiate the peace, this time openly, which paved the way for the Treaty of Utrecht (1713). The settlement extricated England from the conflict, which continued among the remaining comb-atants until 1714 with the Treaty of Rastatt.

Again, the anonymous Dr Swift had made his mark. In *Journal to Stella* (*posth.* 1766), he recounted this hectic period of his life in London. The reign of Queen Anne was reaching its end. In 1713, the same year the Treaty of Utrecht was negotiated to England's considerable advantage, the Queen had been persuaded that Swift's efforts should be recognised; not, though, with a bishop's palace in England as he might have expected, but with the Deanery of St. Patrick's, Dublin. Swift was not really so inclined to return to Ireland, but his days as a player among the power brokers of London were over, and he knew it: he accepted the offer.

In 1714, the last vestige of the Stuart dynasty ended with the death of Queen Anne. The reign of George I commenced, with the return of the Whigs and the protracted tenure of Robert Walpole as First Minister. Those Tory leaders of Swift's acquaintance had now fallen from grace, some had been disgraced, while others faced charges of high treason for conducting secret talks with the French. Robert Harley had been sent to the Tower for a period of reflection. The former Foreign Minister, Lord Bolingbroke, had fled England for exile in Paris. There were those Whigs who had convinced themselves that a Jacobite plot was afoot. The "Old Pretender", so called, might have become James III. As a coverall the Whigs, then, were determined to the secure the Act of Settlement with the Hanoverian succession of George I.

In Ireland again, Dr Jonathan Swift had been transformed into Dean Swift of St. Patrick's Cathedral. As an exile in his own country, or so he felt, he said he was "Like a rat in a hole". As he settled into this new role as Dean,he turned away from London and Europe, and gradually focused his attention on Irish affairs, where he found much to consider.

As a pamphleteer, he was ready to move on, too, and so Swift was about to become highly regarded as a patriot in the land of his birth. In 1720, he produced *Proposal for Use of Irish Manufacture.* The mercantilist policy of the English was sucking the blood out of Ireland, said this pamphleteer. The tract could be counted on to incense those authorities who did not like being lectured to from - of all places - Dublin. The real identity of the author was not difficult to ascertain. Who else but the Dean of St. Patrick's? The authorities, though, proved reluctant to take on someone they knew to have been Queen Anne's pamphleteer. As for the printer, John Harding, that was another matter: he was prosecuted.

In 1724, Swift's most famous or notorious pamphlet appeared with the ironic title: *A Modest Proposal...for Preventing the Poor People in Ireland from being a Burden to their Parents or the Country; and for making them beneficial to the Publick.* The tract is the only of Swift's publications, while he was living, to bear his name. There were those among the public, no doubt, who took Swift - a clergyman bachelor - at his word, and the satirical shock-tactic passed over many heads. Among the gentry, the reaction seems to have been bewilderment or mild amusement, with the ironical reservation "in poor taste". So this is the Dean's real target: the wealthy landlords, who appeared quite indifferent to the human suffering, squalor and degradations in the environs of their grand estates. The broadside, supported by deadly relevant statistics, is generally regarded as a masterpiece of sustained irony. *A Modest Proposal* makes for grizzly reading even today. The poor, he proposed, had an obvious resource in abundance: they should sell their babies as a source of nourishment for the rich, who clearly had no scruples anyway, so cannibalism along class lines offered a practical solution to end poverty for the good of (nearly) all. What was the alternative? Certainly not such extreme measures, the indignant author states, as ". . .teaching landlords to have at least one degree of mercy towards their tenants," as that would be going too far. "Therefore, let no man talk to me of these and the like expedients."

Dean Swift had had his say, with a lacerating wit that seemed to bring a whole class of landowners to its unbending knees. What other motive might Swift have had? He did not write for money, and he never received any money for his pamphlets or books.

The Dean had not yet done with Ireland. In the cycle of seven pamphlets represented by *The Drapier's Letters* (1724-25), the Dean in the guise of "M.B. Drapier" took up the cudgel against a government scheme, approved by Parliament, to introduce a base currency into Ireland in the form of privately minted copper coinage. In the execution of this plan, the licence was awarded by way of letters patent (bought with a bribe of £10,000) to Mr William Wood, an English hardware manufacturer, to produce the coinage for exclusive use in Ireland. The mysterious M.B. Drapier viewed this as one form of corruption leading to another, with all the disastrous consequences implied by the minting of an inferior coinage. As to the identity of the individual (Duchess of Kendall, mistress to King George I) who collected the bribe from Mr Wood, Dean Swift played his hand well (or conserved his ammunition) by remaining discreet. The cycle of *Letters* is variously addressed to: *The Shop-Keepers; Mr Harding the Printer; The Nobility and Gentry; The Whole People of Ireland, Viscount Molesworth;* and *Lord Chancellor Middleton.* The sequence concluded with *An Humble Address to Both Houses of Parliament.*

The British authorities condemned "The Drapier's Letters". The third and fourth 'Letters' even provoked charges of treason against "M. B. Drapier", but it was already far too late: public opinion had turned against the coinage, which was discredited even before its issue. An agitated Robert Walpole withdrew the patent in 1725. The victorious Dean found himself cast in the role of an unlikely hero and "Hibernian patriot": for exposing Mr Wood, standing up to prime minister Robert Walpole and the British government, defying Parliament, and for giving the voiceless a voice. A collected edition of the *Drapier's Letters* was published in 1735.

In these years, since about 1719, Swift had also been working steadily on a book entitled *Travels into Several Remote Regions of the World in Four Parts.* The narrator, Lemuel Gulliver, is First a Surgeon and then a Captain of several ships. After reading passages of the story to servants for a reaction (just imagine their expressions in the candlelight), the long haul was over. Swift took the manuscript to London, his first visit for many years, to arrange for its publication and meet with his old literary friends.

In 1726, when the book appeared with the same elongated title, the tale of the ship's surgeon was a colossal success. This 'international bestseller' would eventually become known to the world as *Gulliver's Travels.*

Swift said that he wrote the book "to vex the world rather than divert it," and he was by now gaining a reputation as something of a (godless) misanthropist.

Those Yahoos were, of course, primarily to blame.

There had, though, always been a certain astringent or wicked playfulness about Swift, not perhaps all that unusual in a clergyman, and this was a highly unusual man of the cloth. For instance, consider the hilarious case of *Partridge versus Bickerstaff* as a cautionary tale for those who would claim foreknowledge of events yet to transpire. Back in 1708, a cobbler by the name of John Partridge had published an almanac of astrological predictions, which included determinations appertaining to the deaths of certain senior clergy. An obscure pamphleteer by the name of Isaac Bickerstaff responded with *Predictions for the Ensuing Year*, which foretold the death of the cobbler Partridge: on the 29 March. On March 30, Bicketstaff published a sequel with the confirmation that the prescient cobbler had indeed expired the day before. When Partridge had attempted to set the record straight, *i.e.*, that he was *not* dead, no one was listening. The unfortunate man, deluded or not, and whatever his ultimate fate, might well have been prescient enough to realise what or who he had been up against. Isaac Bickerstaff was, of course, the *nom do plume* of the Dean

In 1727, Swift made his final journey to London. He stayed with his old friend Alexander Pope, but the visit was curtailed by news of Esther Johnson's illness. Swift returned to Dublin, where he found "Stella" on her deathbed. She passed away on 28 January 1728. Swift preserved a lock of her "black as a raven" hair, but he could not bring himself to attend her funeral.

In 1731, Swift decided to pre-empt his critics by writing his own obituary: *Verses on the Death of Dr Swift,* which was eventually published in 1739 (while he was still alive). A sense of isolation prevailed in these later years, and some of his writings had descended into the scatological realm. By 1742, he was found to have lost the balance of his mind. On 28 October 1745, unable to speak, he eventually died at age seventy-seven. Dean Swift was interred at his own cathedral of St. Patrick's. He left the bulk of his £12,000 estate for the foundation of an insane asylum in Dublin.

A lifetime ago, so it seemed, the Dean had been seated at his desk, trying to write a sermon. Outside the cathedral, a crowd had gathered to watch the eclipse of the sun. The Dean, distracted by the excited chatter, instructed a servant: "Go tell them, I have delayed the eclipse until tomorrow."

Tom Paine,
Revolutionist

IN THE CHRONICLES of the pamphleteers, the case of Tom Paine as an English revolutionary journalist in America and in France is outstanding (and even unlikely). As a staymaker, seaman, then excise man, an encounter with Benjamin Franklin in London propelled Paine on a journey across the Atlantic to work as editor of the fledgling Philadelphia Enquirer. As a working journalist, he also came to write the pamphlet Common Sense, among the most influential pamphlets ever written, and in which he advocated the independence of the American colonies from Britain. In 1776, the timing was perfect, and although the tract "Written by an Englishman" represented high treason, Paine won great fame as a pamphleteer and founding father of the United States of America. The obscure staymaker from Norfolk had come a long way. . .So how, then, did Paine, as a radical of the Enlightenment, end up in on death row of a notorious Parisian prison during the French Revolution, and on his release return to America as a man reviled, his reputation destroyed?

ENGLAND

Thomas Pain(e) was born in Thetford in the English county of Norfolk on 9 February 1737. As the son of Joseph Pain, a staymaker (that is, a corsetmaker) with a shop in Thetford, the course of Paine's life seemed predetermined. A remote figure, Paine's mother Frances was eleven years older than her husband, and appears to have had little or no influence on her son. A second child was born to the Pains, a girl, but she died in infancy. Joseph Pain also had a small farm, and with the extra income derived from this he was able to send his son to the local grammar school, where the Rev. William Knowles served as master.

As Paine grew to maturity, he acquired a sound enough albeit limited level of education. Aged fourteen, he took to his father's trade as an apprentice stay-maker (corsets). After three years of this, the restless streak in his character first emerged, and he ran away to Harwich in an attempt to join the merchant fleet. (In later life, Paine would blame the Rev. Knowles for putting ill-founded ideas into his head.) Joseph Pain apprehended his son at Harwich, and persuaded the sixteen-year-old to return to Thetford. For another three years, Paine continued with the life of a corset-maker. Then, with the outbreak of the Seven Years' War between Britain and France, Paine again escaped the confines of Thetford for the sea. On this occasion, he managed to enlist as an ordinary seaman with the privateer *King of Prussia*.

The Seven Years' War

The Seven Years' War (1756-73) between the European super-powers of the era is usually considered by historians as the earliest international conflict enacted on a global scale. The confrontation involved France, allied with Russia, against Frederich II of Prussia (to whom Britain provided clandestine succour), while France and Britain battled for supremacy in dominions overseas. In the final outcome, Britain achieved supremacy in India; and, with the Peace of Paris in 1763, France ceded Canada and those territories west of the Mississippi (except Louisiana) to Britain while Spain ceded Florida. The war was over, but Britain retained a standing army in defence of the thirteen American colonies, which proved highly expensive. In London, Parliament imposed new direct taxes on the colonies, and this soon led to "no taxation without representation" and the War of American Independence.

Tom Paine's role in the Seven Years' War as an ordinary seaman is a matter of record, but he did not have much to say or write about his service with *King of Prussia* under the command of a Captain Mendez. The details of his naval service have passed mostly unrecorded. Paine spent less than year with the ship. In this time of war, he somehow managed to terminate his service with the *King of Prussia,* and he even collected a bounty for his eight month voyage.

Return to Shore

On his return to shore, he had enough money for an interval in London. This seems to have been an interesting shore leave for Paine, but soon he had stretched his funds to the limit. So he resumed his former trade, but not at Thetford; instead, he found employment with a firm of staymakers based in Hanover Street, London. After less than a year, again he became restless: he moved to Dover for a period, and then on for nearby Sandwich. In 1759, he established his own business as master staymaker. The twenty-two-year old Tom Paine soon found out that he was not much of a businessman. In the September of that year, he married Mary Lambert, a local maid who was the daughter of an erstwhile official with Customs & Excise. When Paine's business failed, the couple moved to Margate, but within a year of her marriage Mary died, possibly during labour, and presumably the baby died with its mother. The episode is obscure, since Paine seems not to have referred to his first wife in his correspondence. Alone again, he decided to adopt his father-in-law's former profession.

Excise Man and Pamphleteer

The decision, once played out, was to be the making of him. In 1761, Paine returned to Thetford to reunite with his parents and make preparations. A recommendation was a perquisite. Once this had been secured, he joined Customs & Excise as a supernumerary officer on 1st December 1762. In this role, he was based in Grantham, where his duties included the inspection of brewers' casks.

In 1764, he was promoted, and charged with the dangerous duty of patrolling the Lincolnshire coastline on the lookout for smugglers. In 1765, Paine was dismissed from his post over his failure to account in the proper way for a consignment. Once again, Paine found himself back in Thetford, employed as a corsetmaker. He endured his old trade until 1767, when he found employment as a teacher of English in London. Soon enough, however, he had been reinstated (after a written apology for his previous oversight) with Customs & Excise. In early 1768, he was posted to Lewes in East Sussex in the capacity of Officer of Excise. By this time, Paine was thirty-one years old, and he had achieved an important rank in a high-risk occupation. Once established in Lewes, he took lodgings with Samuel and Esther Ollive above their fifteenth-century Bull House tobacconists shop. Paine made many influential contacts among the local polity; and, unusually for an outsider, he was even invited to join the Society of Twelve, an elitist club of intellectuals.

In 1769, Samuel Ollive died, survived by his wife Esther, three sons, and a daughter Elizabeth. In respect of the tobacconists, Paine went into partnership with Esther Ollive. In 1771, the thirty-four year old Paine married the Ollive's daughter Elizabeth, who seems to have been under the impression that her charming new husband was

a dedicated bachelor. Then, by 1772, Tom Paine had
settled down to write his first pamphlet. The theme: in
defence of excise men, a group he viewed as engaged in
potentially hazardous work for low wages. The cost of
maintaining a horse, he said, reduced the low income yet
further. The derisory wages, Paine argued, exposed the
excise men to bribery. In Lewes and elsewhere, *bribery*
was something unspoken. The pamphlet entitled *The Case
for Excise Officers* (1772) had a print-run of four thousand
copies, though no doubt Paine incurred a loss. In 1772-73,
he took time away from his post to visit London with copies
of the pamphlet to lobby Members of Parliament, among
others of influence. At this date, he could hardly have
guessed that the pamphlet would act as the catalyst that
would propel him across the Atlantic Ocean to America,
but first there was a heavy price to pay. In 1774, Customs
& Excise dismissed this radical absentee among their
ranks. Paine was now out of work. The Bull House
tobacconists shop had failed. Now a bankrupt, he faced the
prospect of debtors' prison; he managed to sell his
household goods and reached a settlement with his
creditors. In the June of that same year, he separated from
- or abandoned - his wife. Then, he turned his back on
Elizabeth and Lewes forever, and headed for London.

AMERICA

In September 1774, an encounter with the world-famous
Benjamin Franklin, printer and inventor of the lightning
rod, changed the compass of Paine's life. Franklin had
been passing through London as an agent for the
American colonies, and had seen Paine's pamphlet *The
Case for Excise Officers*. A mutual associate made the
introduction, and Franklin encouraged Paine to emigrate

for America. A recent resident of Philadelphia, Franklin provided a letter of recommendation for potential employers in that city. In October of that year, Paine set sail for the colonies.

The voyage across the Atlantic took two months, with landfall made on 30 November 1774. Several passengers were lost to scurvy or typhoid. The ship's drinking water had been contaminated, and when Paine disembarked in Philadelphia he was close to death. He spent his first six weeks ashore in the colonies by way of recuperating. By January 1775, Paine had recovered, to the extent that he was able to secure a temporary position as a tutor. While Franklin's letter might have worked wonders for Paine, a chance encounter in a tavern played its part, too, when he met up with a printer by the name of Robert Aitkin, who had plans for the launch of a periodical. Tom Paine was to be the first managing editor of the *Pennsylvania Magazine*. By this time, with an (e) added to his name, he had adopted citizenship of Pennsylvania. As a journalist, he was found to possess that elusive flair, with a lucid, direct style, and he immersed himself in the affairs of the Americans.

For some years, tensions had been emerging between the British government and the colonists. There was, of course, the question of direct taxation from London: the Navigation Acts, the infamous Stamp Act of 1764 applicable to all printed matter, and so on. A compromise had been reached for a time, with many of these taxes repealed. Then an exception was made: in the very special case of the East India Company - with its grant of a monopoly on tea. . .The mood as quickly changed, and an explosive situation developed: the Boston Tea Party (organised by local vested test interests) took place on 16

December 1773. The first Continental Congress met in Philadelphia in Sept-ember 1774 with a declaration of rights, and the resolution: no imports from Britain, and - unless Britain changed its ways - no exports *to* Britain from the colonies. Soon after, British regulars clashed with Minute Men at Concord and Lexington. In 1775, the second Congress appointed George Washington as commander-in-chief. The Royal Navy imposed a blockade of New England, and so war broke out between Britain and the colonies. France entered the war against Britain in 1778, and the conflict persisted until 1783 with the Treaty of Versailles.

Common Sense

By 1776, Paine had settled into his role as managing editor of the *Pennsylvania Magazine*, with its subscriber base increased threefold to about fifteen hundred. Then, Paine made an extra-ordinary leap into the realm of colonial politics. As a matter of editorial policy, the anodyne *Pennsylvania Magazine* tended to avoid radical political and social issues, even in this time of conflict with Britain. So for his next project Paine resorted once more to the pamphlet form, which he executed with perfect timing: 10 January 1776. This is the date when Paine published the forty-eight page pamphlet originally entitled *The Plain Truth* but then re-titled *Common Sense: Addressed to the Inhabitants of America.* The byline "Written by an Englishman" heightened interest and concealed his identity, since the views expressed were treasonous in the eyes of Britain. The main title of the pamphlet is plain enough, such that the real subject matter is not revealed, and yet the content is on an epic scale: by making the case for American independence from Britain. The tract must be among the most influential ever written, but its real significance is a matter of conjecture. Either way, the pamphlet created an immediate sensation across the thirteen colonies with its two million "free" inhabitants. In the first three months, the pamphlet sold 120,000 copies, with 500,000 in the year of release, and much of the material reprinted in newspaper articles.

The famous sentence: "There is something very absurd in supposing a continent to be perpetually governed by an island," forms part of Paine's case for a break with England. *Common Sense* is considered to have influenced the public debate prior to the third Congress of 4th July 1776, which promulgated the *American Declaration of Independence*, composed by Thomas Jefferson, among others, and signed on 2 August 1776.

Beyond the distant antecedent of *Magna Carta* (*c.* 1215), the primary influences in all of this are John Locke (1632-1704), the English philosopher, and Montesquieu (1689-1755), the French political thinker on the separation of powers. As an outstanding journalist, Paine was able to translate complex ideas into plain language, which remains highly readable (and still relevant) to this day.

> "Society is in every State a blessing, but government, even in its best state, is but a necessary evil."

In this way, the universal themes of *Common Sense* reach out beyond the colonies. Paine's vision of the American Revolution was the futuristic realization (in the here and now) of a benevolent society, where the abuses of power are curtailed and government harnessed for the common good. In advancing his arguments, Paine challenged the very basis of monarchy, and refers in particular to George III as a "Royal Brute". In this era, any expression of contempt for the monarch was taboo, even in the colonies, but Paine - and an Englishman at that - had broken the spell. The radical outspokenness of *Common Sense* infuriated those who remained loyal to Britain. A Maryland loyalist and pamphleteer referred to Paine as "a political quack". Democracy, he assured his readers, is the road to chaos. Among the republican elite, too, there were those, such as James Adams, who thought that this Englishman had shown a lack of restraint with such notions of radical democracy.

The pamphlet had achieved extraordinary sales, but what of a profit? On the first print-run of 1,000 copies, the printer - R. Bell - disclosed that no profit had been made, but Bell continued to print the pamphlet without its author's consent. Paine found another printer, who republished *Common Sense*, with new materials by the anonymous author, and this became established as the *bone fide* version with twenty-five editions in all. Paine insisted that any profits were to be donated to the military effort: by way of mittens for General Washington's soldiers.

The American Crisis

The colonies had severed the tie with Britain, but the war would continue for another seven years. Paine enlisted with the Continental Army in the capacity of secretary and then as *aide-de-camp* to General Nathaniel Greene, who introduced the Englishman to George Washington. In these years of conflict, Paine served the future first President on an occasional basis; and he also produced a series of pamphlets known as *The Crisis,* later collected as

The American Crisis (1776-83). In April 1777, Paine's efforts brought him official recognition with an appointment as secretary to the Congressional Committee on Foreign Affairs. Then as now, this was a political hornets' nest of intrigue. As a journalist, Paine knew too much, and so wrote too much for the liking of the Committee. In one of his articles, he disclosed a confidence (of the French connection), which provided the Committee with exactly the leverage they sought to force Paine out of office. In January 1779, he resigned his post, and eventually picked up 4,000 dollars for his time as secretary (of which he donated 500 dollars for the war effort).

Then, in March 1780, he took up the position of clerk to the Assembly of Pennsylvania, which was the first of the (former) colonies to abolish slavery; not all the assemblies, of course, would follow suit, with the ultimate outcome of conflict between North and South. The prefatory remarks of the anti-slavery Act read very much like the prose of a certain clerk to the Assembly. In this year, too, Paine was provoked into writing the *Public Good* (1780). In this tract, he considered the destiny of the thirteen former colonies - as a whole. The provocation? In a mighty leap of the imagination, Virginia had wanted to extend its borders west - as far as the Pacific seaboard. In doing so, the Virginia Assembly invoked the original King James I Charter of 1609 for the South Virginia Company. In the exercise of such a precedent, Paine foresaw chaos; that is, unless the Congress exerted its will as a union, and for which he proposed the term "United States". The pamphlet, with an outline for a Constitution, provided the Continental Congress with plenty to think about. For Tom Paine, though, the next episode involved a highly unusual diversion, away from the secretarial, into what the

Americans of a later era would come to know as covert operations.

Secret Mission to France

By 1778, France had entered the American War of Independence against Britain, an alliance that proved decisive for the ultimate American victory. In an unusual interlude, even for Paine, he accompanied Col. John Laurens on a top-secret mission to France. In 1781, the expedition set sail with the aim (which was likely Paine's own initiative) to raise finance for the American cause. In England, Tom Paine was *persona non grata*, always with the prospect of charges of high treason brought *in absentia*. In Paris, he was treated as an ally, and he made many high-level contacts that might be reactivated at a later date. The negotiations in the presence of Louis XVI of France were most likely conducted with Benjamin Franklin in attendance (and, if so, imagine Franklin's astonishment at setting eyes on this Englishman once again). King Louis was found to be magnanimous, and a deal was struck: 250,000 livres in silver as a down-payment on a royal 'gift' of 6,000,000 livres with a loan of 10,000,000 livres.[1] In August 1781, Mssrs Laurens and Paine secured return passage across the Atlantic onboard a French warship. On landfall, Tom Paine the famous pamphleteer found himself without gainful employment. After such a mission (which he had undertaken at his own expense) Paine's personal capital had been depleted. In dire need of financial support (and since his services had passed without reward), he turned to an old acquaintance

---

[1] *Life and Writings of Thomas Paine* (Vol 1.) by Daniel Wheeler, pub. Vincent & Clarke, 1908.

for assistance: George Washington referred the matter to Congress, but the initiative faltered, and then ground to a halt - as had, so it seemed, Tom Paine's radical career.

There is another version of this story, however, which seems more probable. Paine had refused payment from the outset, since this was his own initiative (hence he paid his own expenses). Any payment from the Congress for this top-secret mission might have compromised his position, and established a precedent in the vein of mercenary for hire. In any event, Paine had concluded his highly successful mission as *ipso facto* financier to the former colonies. After all, the silver cargo from France had been most welcome, and timely, with the *largesse* of Louis XVI of France used to establish the Bank of North America in January 1782.

Interlude at New Rochelle

The conflict between Britain and its former colonies ended with the Treaty of Paris in 1783. The American War of Independence was over. This same year, Tom Paine made some attempt to settle down with the acquisition of a modest house in New Jersey, which he occupied on and off until his death. Then, in 1784, Tom Paine's unwavering support for the fledgling USA was finally recognised by two of the United States: by the State of New York with a grant of an estate with a fine house and seventy-seven acre farm at New Rochelle; and by the State of Pennsylvania, with a bounty of 500 dollars. Tom Paine, liberated by these benefactors, cast aside long-held financial anxieties to concentrate on his special interests: paper money and an iron bridge.

By the eighteenth century, the issue of paper money had emerged as yet another theme to vex the pamphlet-

teers. As a way to finance the war with Britain, the second
Congress of 1775 had issued the 'Continental' notes, which
were soon worth next to nothing. A decade later, when new
efforts were afoot by the Pennsylvania Assembly to
engineer an increase in the amount of paper notes in
circulation, Paine's 1786 pamphlet *Dissertations on
Government* included a vitriolic attack on the currency,
which, he reminded his readers, is not money, but merely
promissory notes - or paper with a promise. "Paper notes,"
he fulminated, "given and taken between individuals is
one thing, but paper issued by an Assembly *as* money is
another thing" - an *apparition.* Paine's words retain a
certain resonance in the present era:

> "Money when considered as the fruit of many years'
> industry, as the reward of labour, sweat and toil, as
> the widow's dowry and the children's portion, and
> as the means of procuring the necessities of and
> alleviating the afflictions of life, and making old age
> as a scene of rest, has something in it sacred that is
> not to be sported with, or trusted to the airy bubble
> of paper money."

In this interlude at the La Rochelle farm, Tom Paine had
other matters on his mind besides mere paper: iron, and
especially an iron bridge, a project that would bring him
once more across the Atlantic to Europe.

A Bridge to Europe

The world's first iron bridge with a single-span of 100 ft.
had been constructed on the River Severn in 1779. Tom
Paine's design (inspired by a spider's web) for an iron
bridge was more ambitious, with a span three-to-five times
that of the Severn endeavour. For technical support, he

enlisted the services of mechanic John Hall, an émigré from Leicester, and the Walker Brothers as manufacturers based in Rotherham, Yorkshire. By 1787, Paine had again become restless; this was more than enough to inspire him to undertake the voyage to France and England in search of a showcase for his bridge design. As he travelled between Paris and London, Paine seems to have been unconcerned as to how the British authorities might react to his visit in view of the "Royal Brute" insult and his previous career as revolutionist in America. The visit, though, seems to have passed without incident. In the May of that year, he exhibited a model of his bridge in Paris, but to no avail.

On his return to England, he travelled to Thetford for a reunion with his parents, only to discover that his father had passed away. Paine made financial arrangements for his elderly mother, but she did not live long enough to appreciate the support of her famous son. In December, he returned to Paris to meet with a former associate: Thomas Jefferson, who was by then US Ambassador to France. Jefferson might well have been bemused by Paine's plans for an iron bridge. And what of the bridge? A more modest, scaled-down affair had been erected near Paddington, London. There was, of course, always the original model version: this would serve as the basis for the Schuylkill River Bridge in Pennsylvania and the Sunderland Bridge on the River Wear in England. By this time, though, Paine's thoughts had already strayed from his original mission to Europe. In France, times had changed since his secret journey there in 1781. In December 1787, when Paine had met with Jefferson, King Louis XVI remained on the throne of France, with the Marie Antoinette at his side, but not for much longer. Revolution was in the air.

Fig. 27 Tom Paine (1737-1809): an unlikely career as Thetford corset-maker, for a time seaman in the Seven Years War, Lewes excise man, then propagandist for the revolutions in American and France. In the wayward tradition of pamphleteering, *The Age of Reason* (1794) exploded in his face, and assured his undoing. Painting (1880): Auguste Millière. *Courtesy: National Portrait Gallery, London.*

Fig. 28 Benjamin Franklin (1706-1790): famous American and inventor of the lightning rod, who encouraged Paine to emigrate to the colonies. After a hazardous two-month voyage, Paine found work as the editor of the *Pennsylvania Magazine.*

Painting (c. 1785.): Joseph Duplessis. Courtesy NPG, London.

Fig. 29 *(over) Common Sense* (1776): "Written by an Englishman", barely a year after Paine's arrival in the colonies, the anonymous 48-page pamphlet made the case (with perfect timing) for American independence from Britain. The tract sparked a public debate prior to the third Congress of 4 July 1776 and the *Declaration of Independence.* A sensation across the thirteen colonies, the pamphlet sold 120,000 copies in the first three months alone, with 25 editions in all.

Paine was viewed by many loyalists as a dangerous radical.

Image: first edition. The printer R. Bell reported sales of 1,000 copies - with no profit. Printers have not changed as much as their technology. Paine soon found another printer.

George Nelson

COMMON SENSE;

ADDRESSED TO THE

INHABITANTS

O F

A M E R I C A,

On the following interesting

S U B J E C T S.

I. Of the Origin and Design of Government in general,
with concise Remarks on the English Constitution.

II. Of Monarchy and Hereditary Succession.

III. Thoughts on the present State of American Affairs.

IV. Of the present Ability of America, with some mis-
cellaneous Reflections.

Man knows no Master save creating HEAVEN,
Or those whom choice and common good ordain.
THOMSON.

PHILADELPHIA;
Printed, and Sold, by R. BELL, in Third-Street.
MDCCLXXVI.

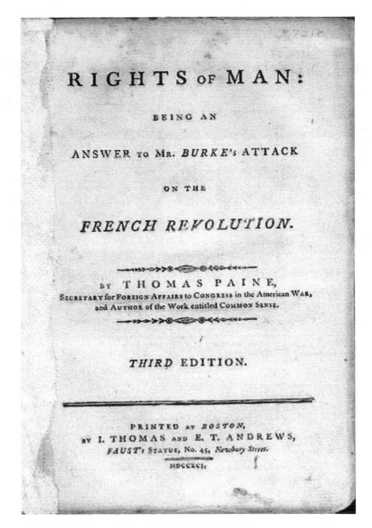

Fig. 30 *Rights of Man* (1791 & 92): Paine's counter-attack on Edmund Burke's denunciation of the French Revolution. There were those, Paine wrote, who "feared the example of France in England". In 1792, France was proclaimed a republic. In 1793, Louis XVI was executed, and so began the Reign of Terror.

Fig. 31 Edmund Burke (1729-1797): the British statesman's *Reflections on the French Revolution* (1792) by way of "A Letter to a Frenchman" denounced the violent events in Paris, with the advice: "reform, not revolution". France, he said, was a "country undone". His 'Letter' was answered, not by a Frenchman, but by an Englishwoman. *Painting:* Sir *Joshua Reynolds (c. 1767-69). Courtesy: National Portrait Gallery, London.*

Fig. 32 Mary Wollstonecraft (1759-1797): she aimed, she said, to be the "first of a new genus." Mary responded to Burke with *Vindication of the Rights of Men* (1790), which predates Paine's *Rights of Man* (1791-92), and paved the way for her revolutionary pamphlet *Vindication of the Rights of Woman* (1792). *Painting*: John Opie (*c.* 1797). *Courtesy: National Portrait Gallery, London.*

THE

AGE

OF

REASON;

BEING

AN INVESTIGATION

OF

TRUE AND FABULOUS THEOLOGY.

BY THOMAS PAINE,

SECRETARY FOR FOREIGN AFFAIRS TO CONGRESS
IN THE AMERICAN WAR,

AND AUTHOR OF THE WORKS ENTITLED,

COMMON SENSE, AND RIGHTS OF MAN, &c.

PARIS:
PRINTED BY BARROIS.

LONDON: Sold by D. I. EATON, at the COCK AND SWINE,
No. 74, Newgate-ftreet.

1794.

PRICE TWO SHILLINGS.

Fig. 33 *The Age of Reason* (1794-95): composed by Paine
prior to ('94), and after ('95), his imprisonment at the
Luxembourg in Paris. An investigation of the Biblical
account, the pamphlet exploded in Paine's face, and assured
his undoing. The subtitle invites as much. For the many
credulous readers of this era, Paine had gone too far.

THE FRENCH REVOLUTION

The French Revolution, with its roots in an outmoded system of feudal governance, was triggered by the clash of the heavily taxed *bourgeoisie* (the third estate) with the clergy (the first estate) and the aristocracy (the second estate). By May 1789, the country had embarked on a course that would end the *ancien régime*, and which opened the way for the dictatorship of Bonaparte in 1799 and the era of the Napoleonic Wars.

5 May 1789 *Louis XVI convenes the old Estates-General (États généraux: that is, the feudal assembly of the three estates) to debate the fiscal predicament (exacerbated by support for the American Revolution) and the urgent need for economic reform. Members of the third estate decided to meet independently as the Communes.*
17 June 1789 *The Communes proclaim the National Assembly in defiance of the ruling elite.*
9 July 1789 *The National Assembly is reconstituted as the National Constituent Assembly.*
14 July 1789 *The Parisian mob, led by pamphleteer Camille Desmoulins, storms the Bastille in search of arms.*

In Paris, with the fall of the Bastille, the balance of power had shifted dramatically, such that Louis XVI now recognised the new Constituent Assembly (in place of the National Assembly). The Constituent Assembly asserted the *Declaration of the Rights of Men* as the foundations of the Revolution, with plans for a restricted monarchy. Louis XV1 eventually accepted the constitution, but the remote King Louis and his advisers had lost touch with the people long ago. The slogan of the revolutionists: "Liberty, Fraternity and Equality". In Paris, radical political clubs, such as the Jacobins, began to emerge. For the nobility, the signs were of deep foreboding, and there were those who decided to flee Paris while they still had the chance.

Rights of Man

In the way of such things, Tom Paine had travelled to France to promote his design for a single-span iron bridge, and yet he came to exert an influence on the French Revolution. Even after the storming of the Bastille, led by pamphleteer Camille Desmoulins on 14 July 1789, the iron bridge remained as Paine's top priority (and this is reflected in his correspondence with Jefferson). A recent acquaintance, though, provided a timely distraction. In 1790, the British statesman Edmund Burke (1729-1797) published *Reflections on the French Revolution*, a condemnation of the violent events then taking place across the Channel. Of Burke, the record should be set straight: it is often recorded that he was all for the American Revolution and against the French Revolution. For the colonies, Edmund Burke advised *reconciliation*, not revolution. In a speech to Parliament on 19 April 1774, Burke warned of the levy on tea: "Leave America, if she has taxable matter in her, to tax herself...Be content to bind America by laws of trade." Then again, on 22 March 1775: "[the colonists] are descendants of Englishmen. They are therefore not only devoted to liberty, but to liberty according to English ideas. . ." On the American Revolution, Burke's view is expressed in the same terms as a justifiable reassertion of those rights already established under the British Constitution. These are, of course, the words of a Whig statesman, a liberal conservative as might be said, and not a revolutionist like Paine. As for the tumultuous events in France, Burke foresaw dire consequences. *Reflections* is written in the form of a "Letter to a Frenchman" with advice on the way ahead: reform, not revolution. "A country undone," is how he described France at this time. A prompt reply to Burke's "Letter" came, not from a Frenchman, but an Englishwoman.

IN THAT SAME year, Mary Wollstonecraft (1759-97) published *Vindication of the Rights of Men* (thus pre-dating Paine's response) with its title reflecting the *Declaration* of the French Assembly. For Mary, who advocated republicanism, and away with the aristocracy, *Vindication* attracted international recognition. As well as an account of the early days of the French Revolution, Mary went on to publish her acclaimed *Vindication of the Rights of Woman* (1792); this is among the earliest tracts looking at the status of women in society and the preconceptions of the era. She was, she asserted, aiming to become "the first of a new genus".

In London again, Tom Paine produced his *Rights of Man* (1791-92) "...*Being an Answer to Mr. Burke's Attack on the French Revolution*". The pamphlet was published in London on 13 March 1791, and Paine soon attracted the special interest of the authorities. "Certain other persons," he had written, "now feared the example of the French Revolution in England."

The first part of *Rights of Man* is dedicated to George Washington. Paine takes aim, and the opening salvo finds its target: "Among the incivilities by which nations or individuals provoke and irritate each other, Mr. Burke's pamphlet on the French Revolution is an extraordinary instance." Paine went on to say of Burke: "It is painful to behold a man employing his talents to corrupt himself."

In defending the Revolution, Paine explores, with great clarity of style, the nature of absolute monarchy *versus* representative government; and since government, he argues, is a *contract* with the people, then revolution is justifiable when government interferes with the rights of the people. On rights:

> "Natural rights are those that appertain to man in rights of his existence."

On those who would seek to control posterity:

> "The vanity and presumption of governing beyond the grave is the most ridiculous and insolent of all tyrannies."

On the significance of the Bastille:

> "The Bastille was to be either the prize or the prison of the assailants. The downfall of it included the idea of the downfall of Despotism..."

On the position of King Louis XVI:

> "It was not against Louis XVIth, but against the despotic principles of government, that the nation revolted. These principles had not their origin in him, but in the establishment many centuries back. . . ."

On the restraint of the National Assembly:

> "Whom has the National Assembly brought to the scaffold? None."

In France, though, events continued to unfold. In 1791, Burke's pamphlet *A Letter to a Member of the National*

Assembly urged counter-revolution by external forces for the "undoing" of the Revolution, but by this stage unstoppable political forces had already been unleashed.

20-21 June 1791 *Louis XVI and his family attempt escape. Louis is recognised at Varennes. The Royal family is escorted back to Paris and placed under house arrest.*
30 September 1791 *National Constituent Assemely dissolved.*
1 October 1791 *The Legislative Assembly is proclaimed.*

In February 1792, Tom Paine issued *Rights of Man, Part the Second*, which he dedicated to M. de Lafayette. Essentially, the tract elucidates principles drawn from the original pamphlet, with some conclusions. Paine even considers such epic themes as "Society and Civilization".

On the real significance of the American Revolution:

> "The independence of America, considered merely as a separation from England, would have been a matter of but little importance, had it not been accompanied by a revolution in the principles and practice of governments."

On progressive taxation:

> "Invention is continually exercised to furnish new pretences for revenue and taxation. It watches prosperity as its prey, and permits none to escape without a tribute."

On society (and government):

> " . . .society performs for itself almost everything ascribed to it by government. . ."

> ". . .government is nothing more than a national
> association acting on the principles of society."

Rights of Man continues with "Of the Old and New
Systems of Governments", followed by "Of Constitutions".

Paine concludes his treatise with 'Ways and Means' in
which he even finds the space to elucidate his futuristic
vision for social security with a national pension scheme.
In a far-sighted vision of how conditions in Europe might
be improved. He states:

> "It is time nations should be rational, and nor be
> governed like animals, for the pleasure of their
> riders..."

Power, he seems to say, serves only itself, and with no
other end. Paine leaves his readers with a flourish:

> " Thus wishing as I sincerely do, freedom and
> happiness to all nations, I close. . ."

In the combined edition, *Rights of Man* sold in the region
of 200,000 copies. The first part had sold well enough, but
its impact had been limited: with the debunking of Burke
and ridicule of the madness of the heredity principle
(George III had been 'barking' at this interlude), the tract
had passed without much in the way of controversy. The
second part, with its assault on government, was another
matter. The Prime Minister of the day, William Pitt, seems
to have taken exception to Paine and his pamphlet. The
British government now considered Paine as a threat to
the national interest.

By May 1792, the charge of seditious libel had been
levelled against the author and printer. A campaign was

soon under way to discredit Paine. A warrant had been issued for the arrest of the famous pamphleteer, and so Paine was persuaded on the course of exile. Once again, he made the Channel crossing from Dover to Calais, and then onwards for Paris.

TOM PAINE IN PARIS

In the European arena, the convulsions within France had un-settled arch enemies. In 1792, France declared war on Austria, and war with Prussia followed within months. In the military campaign, the Revolutionary armies suffered early reversals. As Austrian troops approached the French capital, Parisians became fearful. The nobility was, in the angry eyes of the Parisian mob, suspected of complicity with the enemies of France abroad, and reprisals followed with the massacres of September 1792.

20 September 1992 *The Legislative Assembly is dissolved. The National Convention is formed, with such radicals as Maximilien de Robespierre, Georges Danton[1], the always-angry Jean-Paul Marat[2], and the unlikely foreigner Tom Paine, et. al.*

The first act of the National Convention was to abolish the monarchy. The Convention, though, made up of the

---

[1] A national hero to this day, the Le Danton café is to be found on the boulevard Saint Germain in Paris. Any sign of a café Robespierre in this city or anywhere else is most unlikely.

[2] As for M. Marat, with his revolutionary periodical *L'Ami du peuple*, he must be among the angriest, as well as the most influential, newspaper editors in history; he was assassinated in his bathtub, where he spent much time as a palliative for a persistent skin condition.

various political clubs - the Girondins, Montagnards, and so on - soon found itself hamstrung by internal discord.

An exile from England, Paine arrived in Calais to a hero's welcome, and reached Paris on 19 September 1792 as an honorary citizen of France (who was unable to speak French). In England, Paine was regarded as a dangerous radical, but in France he was viewed as a moderate. A natural ally of the Girondins, he was elected to the Convention as the representative of the Pas-de-Calais district. In England, Paine's exalted rank in France translated to the status of traitor at home, and he had since been charged with seditious libel over *Rights of Man* and tried *in absentia*. Away across the Channel, he responded: "If these things be libellous, then let the name of the libeller be engraved on my tomb."

In his capacity as representative to the Convention, he voted in favour of the proclamation of France as a republic on 22 September 1792, but he was against the execution of Louis XVI (exile to America would, Paine proposed, be preferable). There were those among the Convention, though, who did not view the world in the same light as this foreign interloper with the too much influence over the affairs of France.

The Luxembourg

As the people of France looked into the abyss, the Reign of Terror was about to commence. By 1793, Paine was in serious jeopardy of the extremists. The balance of power in the Convention had shifted away from the Girondins and towards the Montagnards and the Jacobins. Robespierre, especially vindictive and dangerous, had no time for Paine. In December 1793, the Convention passed a motion prohibiting 'foreigners' from the assembly. As an ally of the

Girondins, Paine was ejected from the Convention, arrested, and imprisoned at the Luxembourg.

21 January 1793 *Louis XVI is charged with treason and executed by guillotine.*
6 April 1793 *The Convention establishes the Committee of Public Safety with Robespierre as virtual dictator of France.*

THE EXILE Paine had placed himself in an impossible situation: an Englishman, who was an American citizen and revolutionary hero, who was an honorary citizen of France, who had spoken up for the life of Louis XVI. Now, Louis was dead and Paine stared death in the face. An ally might have been expected in the person of the US Ambassador to Paris, but a certain Gouverneur Morris had replaced Thomas Jefferson in that capacity in 1789. Paine had been unaware that he had a jealous enemy in Morris, who thought him an uneducated commoner and an upstart. The inaction of Morris, and his probable connivance (with Robespierre) in the arrest, meant that Paine languished at the Luxembourg. Where were his powerful allies now? Paine convinced himself that George Washington, while seeking to improve relations with the British, had abandoned him to the bloody hands of the Terrorists. Another, more charitable slant on the Gouverneur Morris affair suggests that the diplomat considered the high-profile Paine in the Luxembourg as out of sight, and so out of danger. (An unworldly person might even believe that account.) As an alibi if needed, the pretence was convincing · for as long as Paine remained alive. As the months passed, Paine's escape from the guillotine appears to have been a close shave indeed, with no credit to the ostensibly devious Morris. On one occasion, a guard had passed through the Luxembourg with the purpose of marking white crosses on the doors of those prisoners who were to be executed the next day. That same night, the door of Paine's cell had been opened for ventilation; the guard had marked the door with chalk. The door was then closed during the night, such that the white cross was visible only on the inside · and to which Paine, presumably, awoke. The incident is like something out of Alexander Dumas; but, whatever the actuality, Paine survived while the guillotine outside · the "National Razor" · continued to process those selected by the *Committee of Public Safety*.

By the time of Paine's arrest at the Hotel Philadelphia in the early hours of 29 December 1793, an "Autobiographical Interlude" reveals that had already completed the first part of a new pamphlet, which he had then passed to an associate in the event of his arrest.

The Age of Reason

In Paine's career as a pamphleteer he had investigated themes on an epic scale. In Paris, his thoughts then turned to the greatest of all themes with matters of a theological dimension. *The Age of Reason* is considered a work of *deism*, that is to say, related to the belief in an omniscient creator who does not intervene in creation or human affairs; whereas, *theism* is the belief in god(s) as creator who intervenes in creation and human affairs.

In *The Age of Reason*, Paine had effectively launched a single·handed assault on organized religion, which he considered a subject, as with any subject, for open·minded enquiry, and hence the title with its Enlightenment perspective. In doing so, Paine challenged some of the basic tenets of the Christian faith, while, for evidence, he interrogated the biblical account for consistency. The subtitle of the pamphlet is enough to antagonize the pious (and the not so pious): *Being an Investigation of the True Fabulous Theology.*

9 Thermidor (Revolutionary calendar) or 27 July 1794
Maximilien de Robespierre is overthrown in a coup d'etat by the Convention.

AFTERMATH AND INFAMY
At the US Embassy in Paris, James Munro (who had replaced Gouverneur Morris) exerted his considerable influence on behalf of Paine as an American citizen. As a British citizen, Paine's execution, however that might be accomplished, had apparently been scheduled for September 1794. Paine had been tried *in absentia*, and now he faced, in some bizarre symbolic way, execution *in absentia* - an indication, surely, as to the extent the British government feared Paine's influence.

In November 1794, after eleven months at the Luxembourg, Paine was released. A free man again, he elected to stay on in Paris. As a guest at the house of James Munroe, he set to work on the second part of *The Age of Reason.* By July 1795, he had been reinstated as a member of the Convention with its new Constitution (which he voted against as undemocratic). In October of that year, the combined version of *The Age of Reason* appeared. The outcry has not yet really ceased.

*

18 November 1795 *After the execution of Robespierre, a new Constitution is adopted with the establishment of the Directory. The way is opened for the Consulate under Napoleon Bonaparte in November 1799.*

THE NEW CENTURY opened with the dictatorship of Bonaparte. Of Napoleon and Tom Paine, there is something to say, although this might only be the tabletalk of Paine's many enemies. In the year 1800, the anecdote relates of an unlikely encounter between the exiled Englishman and the Corsican to discuss plans for the invasion of England. The story is embellished with remarks by Napoleon: that he slept with a copy of *Rights of Man* under his pillow; that a "gold statue of Paine should be erected in every city of the world". The anecdote of this dangerous liaison may well be apocryphal, but at least some tangible evidence survives with Paine's two essays on the subject of invasion.

As for Bonaparte, Paine came to change his mind: "The completest scoundrel that ever existed."

In 1802, with the support of Thomas Jefferson, Paine left France forever and sailed for the United States. In Baltimore, the prospect of a hero's welcome seemed unlikely. After his endeavours in England, America and in France, the corsetmaker turned revolutionist ended his days as a man reviled, his reputation destroyed, and abandoned by those who had once admired him. In publishing *The Age of Reason*, Paine's reveals a naive streak; and perhaps his instincts as a journalist had deserted him. After what he had been through, he must have guessed that if some people might misunderstand his motives, then there were those, too, who would go out of their way to misunderstand him.

If *Common Sense* had been treason in British eyes, then there were many who saw *The Age of Reason* as nothing less than sacrilege. There is yet more to account for Paine's infamy, though, since many Americans would not, and could not, bring themselves to forgive Paine's remarks in his open letter to George Washington: "The world will be puzzled to decide whether you are an apostate or an impostor."

In such ways, Tom Paine the radical democrat came to be resented as a zealot, a drunkard, an atheist, and (in England) a traitor. Tom Paine's real achievement had been to develop a highly effective political journalism, forensic in its method, radical in its purpose, free of cant, readable to this day, with that rare touch, and an influence that persists.

On 8 June 1809, Paine died aged seventy-two in the reduced circumstances of a brandy soak at Greenwich Village, New York. A church burial on consecrated ground refused, Paine's body was interred on his New Rochelle farm in New York, where a memorial now stands. In 1819, the British journalist William Cobbet took the initiative with a plan to ship Paine's remains back to England, but the bones somehow went missing on the voyage.

There is, though, a vestigial remnant of that remark attributed to Napoleon Bonaparte. In Paris, the people of the city erected a gold-plated statue to the memory of Tom Paine in the Parc Montsouris by the Cité Universitaire:

Citoyen du Monde

Citizen of the World.

Bibliography

AYER, A. J.: *Thomas Paine*, faber & faber, London, 1989

BENÉNT, William Rose: *Reader's Encyclopaedia, The* (4th Ed.)
    Ed. by Bruce Murphy, A & C Black, London, 1998

BROGAN, Hugh: *History of the United States of America*,
    Penguin (*orig*. Longman, 1985), London, 1990

BURGESS, Anthony: *Shakespeare*, Jonathan Cape, London, 1970

DILLON, Janette: *Early English Theatre*, Cambridge University
    Press, 2006

FOAKES, R. A., Editor. *Henslowe's Diary* (2nd edition),
    Cambridge University Press, 2002.

FROST, William: "Dryden and Satire", essay *in the Journal
    Studies in English Literature (1500-1900)*, No. 3, Vol II,
    Summer 1971, Rice University, Texas, USA, 1971

GLENDINNING, Victoria: *Jonathan Swift*, Pimlico, London, 1999

HORNE, Sir Alistair: *La Belle France*, Vintage Books, USA, 2006
    London, 1940

MURPHY, Bruce: *The Reader's Encyclopaedia* (Fourth Edition),
    A & C Black, London, 1998

PAINE, Thomas: *Rights of Man*, Dover Publications, Inc.,
    Mineola, New York, 1999

RHYS, Ernest (Ed.): *Thomas Dekker*, Ernest Benn Ltd., London
    1949

WILSON, A.N.: *The Life of John Milton*, Oxford University
    Press, 1983

WELLS, Stanley: *Thomas Nashe, Selected Works*, Edward
    Arnold Ltd., London, 1964

WEST, Richard: *The Life and Strange, Surprising Adventures of
    Daniel Defoe*, Flamingo, London, 1998

Further Reading

BROGAN, Hugh: *The Penguin History of the United States of America,* 2nd Rev. Edition, Penguin, London, 2001.

GRIFFITHS, Denis: *Fleet Street: 500 Years of the Press,* British Library Publishing, 2006

HOBSAWM, E. J.: *The Age of Revolution: Europe 1789-1848,* Cardinal, London, 1962

HORNE, Sir Alistair: *La Belle France,* Vintage Books, USA, reprint 2006.

ORWELL, George & Reynolds, Reginald: *British Pamphleteers,* 2 Vols., A. Wingate, London, 1948

ORWELL, George: "Pamphlet Literature" (1943) in *Collected Essays, Letters and Journalism of George Orwell Vol. 2 (1940-43),* Penguin, London, 1971

RAYMOND, Joad: *Pamphlets and Pamphleteering in early Modern Britain,* Cambridge University Press, 2003

MCCRUM, Robert with MacNeil, Robert and McKay, Janet Holmgren: *The Story of English* (new edition), faber & faber, London, 2002

MCLUAN, Marshall: *The Gutenberg Galaxy: The Making of Typographic Man,* University of Toronto Press, 1962

WATSON, Patrick & Barber, Benjamin: *Struggle for Democracy, The,* W. H. Allen, London, 1990.

Information & links
Bibliographic data and ongoing research
www.thepamphleteers.com

General
British Library
www.bl.org

Incunabula: short title catalogue
International database of 15th century
European printing
www.data.cerl.org/istc/

Library of Congress
Rare Book and Special Collections
www.loc.gov/rr/rarebook/
{refer Radical Pamphlet Collection}

World Digital Library
[LOC and UNESCO]
www.wdl.org/en/

Bibliothèque nationale de France
www.bnf.fr

Folger Library
Breaking News · Birth of the Newspaper
[exhibit 2008-09]
www.folger.edu

Cambridge History of English & American Literature
(Pamphleteers)
www.bartleby.com

Luminarium:
Anthology of English Literature
[Greene, Dekker, Nashe, *et. al.*]
www.luminarium.org

Elizabethan Authors
www.elizabethanauthors.com

The Gutenberg Project
www.gutenberg.org
[Online texts by numerous pamphleteers,
including full text of Milton's *Areopagitica*]

Collections

19th Century British pamphlets
{Uni. of Birmingham/Univ. of Liverpool consortium}
www.britishpamphlets.org.uk

The Simpson Collection
{Royal College of Physicians of Edinburgh}
www.rcpe.ac.uk/heritage/

University of Liverpool
[Special Collections and Archives]
www.liverpool.ac.uk/library

Daniel Defoe

Digital Defoe
www.english.illinoisstate.edu/digitaldefoe/

Lilly Library Collection
{University of Indiana}
www.indiana.edu/~liblilly/defoe/

John Milton

Citizen Milton
www.cems.ox.ac.uk/citizenmilton/

Tom Paine

Tom Paine Project
www.tompainelewes.org.uk

Tom Paine Society
www.thomaspainesociety.org

Jonathan Swift & Daniel Defoe
Monash University Library
www.lib.monash.edu.au/exhibitions/swift-defoe

Index

Cont'd. over . . .

CPSIA information can be obtained
at www.ICGtesting.com
Printed in the USA
LVHW05s1952181018
594041LV00019B/980/P

9 780955 183447